Teachers' Template Collection for Microsoft® Office™

Intermediate

Editor
Kathy Humrichouse

Project Editor
Paul Gardner

Editor-in-Chief
Sharon Coan, M.S. Ed.

Art Director
Elayne Roberts

Cover Artist
Denise Bauer

Product Manager
Phil Garcia

Imaging
Alfred Lau

Acknowledgements

Microsoft® Office™ Software is ©1991–2000 Microsoft Corporation. All Rights Reserved. *Microsoft® Office™* is a trademark of Microsoft Corporation, registered in the U. S. and other countries. Microsoft, Clip Art ©1997. All rights reserved..

Trademarks

All brand names and product names used in this book are trade names, service marks, trademarks, or registered trademarks of their respective owners. Teacher Created Resources, Inc. is not associated with any product or vendor mentioned in this book.

Publisher
Mary D. Smith, M.S. Ed.

Authors

Javier Martinez and Joseph K. Robinson

Teacher Created Resources, Inc.
6421 Industry Way
Westminster, CA 92683
www.teachercreated.com

ISBN: 978-1-57690-771-9

©2000 Teacher Created Resources, Inc.
Reprinted, 2007
Made in U.S.A.

The classroom teacher may reproduce copies of materials in this book for classroom use only. The reproduction of any part for an entire school or school system is strictly prohibited. No part of this publication may be transmitted, stored, or recorded in any form without written permission from the publisher.

Table of Contents

Introduction 4

Using this Template Collection to Design and Build Portfolios 5

Installation 6

Teacher Templates for Microsoft Word® 8

Seating Chart Templates 9

Student Awards 13

    Teacher Documents 21

        Inventory Sheet 21

        Classroom Management Plan 22

        Classroom Supply List 23

        Student Trip 23

        School Rules 24

        Discipline Notice to Parents 24

        Letter Home 25

        Homework Assignments 25

        Letterheads 26

        Memo Samples 27

        Teacher Business Cards 28

        Notes and Ideas for Substitute 29

        Week at a Glance 30

        Maps 31

        Social Studies Curriculum Connections 39

    Student Templates 43

        Daily Journal 44

        Personal Journal 44

        Vocabulary Word List 45

        Daily Schedule 46

        My Story 47

        Student Reports 48

        Study Buddies 50

    Science Templates

        The Human Hand 51

        The Human Brain 52

        Digestive System 53

        The Human Lungs 54

        The Human Heart 55

Table of Contents (cont.)

Science Templates (cont.)
- The Human Skull 56
- The Environment 56
- Computer Technology 57
- The Microscope 58
- Molecules 59
- Liquids 60
- Rocket Technology 60
- Space Exploration 61
- Scientific Instruments 62

Teacher Templates for Microsoft PowerPoint® 63

Teacher Presentation Templates
- Open House Presentation 65
- Student Awards Presentation 69
- Department Resource Presentation 72

Lesson Presentation Template (Oceans) 74

Lesson Presentation Template (Social Studies) 75

Student Presentation Templates
- Family Tree Presentation 77
- A Day at the Zoo Presentation 79
- Storybook Maker Presentation 81
- Study Guide Presentation 83
- Electronic Yearbook Presentation 86

Teacher Templates for Microsoft Excel® **94**

Teacher Templates
- Grade Book 95
- Lesson Plan Spreadsheet for Teachers 98
- Seating Charts 99

Student Templates
- Math Worksheets 100
- Student Planner for Students 102

Teacher Templates for Microsoft Access® 103
- Student Information System 103

Teacher Templates for Microsoft Binder® 108

Index of CD-ROM Files 109

Introduction

The *Teacher's Template Collection for Microsoft Office* is a collection of templates that teachers and students can use on a daily basis. All of the templates are designed using *Microsoft Office*. A teacher using this collection will find a variety of templates that will facilitate classroom management and maintenance. The grade book and lesson plan template will assist the teacher who might need to quickly calculate student grades or to reference the school schedules. *Microsoft Office* provides users with many additional useful templates.

This book is divided into three sections that contain templates created by the three applications in *Microsoft Office: Microsoft Word, Microsoft PowerPoint,* and *Microsoft Excel.* Each of these sections is then divided again into two sections, templates for teachers and templates for students. For the Windows version are templates created by *Microsoft Binder.* A Sample *Microsoft Access* Student/School Database is also included.

The *Microsoft Word* section of this book contains templates for the following uses and more:

- Seating Charts
- Maps
- Classroom Management Plan
- Discipline Notice to Parents
- Student Awards
- Voyages to the Past
- School Rules
- Letters Home for Parents

The *Microsoft PowerPoint* section contains templates for a variety of topics that will allow the user to create fun and meaningful multimedia presentations. These include:

- Open House
- Department Personnel Information with course overviews

Microsoft Excel templates consist of a grade book and a lesson plan chart for teachers. There are a variety of Math template worksheets for students. Automatic scoring on the computer will allow the student to self-correct homework and class assignments.

The Student Information Database is a template created with *Microsoft Access* and is a unique database program. Teachers can also modify this template and use *Microsoft Access* to build student schedules and maintain teacher assignments and profiles. Another feature includes an easy overview of student grades, schedules and progress reports. *Microsoft Access* can be run on your school-wide network.

Using This Template Collection to Design and Build Portfolios

Portfolio assessment, when used as an evaluation tool, can be easily managed with the use of a computer and *Microsoft Office*. When you look at the objectives of portfolio use, everything needed to represent a collection of work done over a period of time can be created and managed with the use of these templates and *Microsoft Binder*. The Binder program has a unique way of assembling work files into electronic folders. Work samples can then be stored easily by the date they were created and progress can be evaluated over time. Some sample Binders have been created and included on the CD-ROM to illustrate the power of the Binder Program.

With the *Student Planner Binder,* each student can create and maintain his own "personal learning plan." This is a powerful extension to add to the portfolio process. Students can better understand what expectations they must meet when goals and objectives are established at the start of the school year. Instructors can use this personal learning planner to make students accountable for their performance. Each student can sign a learning contract that states he understands the course objectives and what must be accomplished. He then forms an agreement with the instructor regarding his expected level of performance. With planning added to the learning process, students can better understand what is expected of them each day at school.

Teachers also have access to planning tools that make this template collection a highly effective program by saving them time. The Teacher Template Binder is a set of templates designed just for teachers. It includes templates for lesson planning, a grade book spreadsheet, and other documents that are core activities teachers do most often.

With this wide assortment of templates, you can create student portfolios that can be used across the curriculum. There are numerous templates for the areas of language arts, mathematics, science, and social science. Different combinations of templates can be collected and placed into Microsoft Binders to build very unique portfolios.

When you look at how this vast collection of templates works, you will discover that you have all of the tools within *Microsoft Office* that you would find if you were combining the leading teacher tool products. *Teachers' Templates for Microsoft Office* shows you how to use *Microsoft Office* as a worksheet generator, a grade book program, a lesson plan program, and a portfolio assessment program.

Installing and Using Templates with Windows

There are two options with which to use these templates on your computer.

Option One: Opening Templates from the CD-ROM

The easiest way to use this collection is to open the templates directly from the CD-ROM. The drawback to this method is that you must insert the CD-ROM whenever you wish to use a template. To open templates directly from the CD-ROM, complete the following steps:

1. Double-click the My Computer icon on the desktop in windows.
2. Next double-click the CD-ROM icon located in the folder My Computer.
3. Select the file you wish to use and double-click it.
4. To save any of your changes simply select *Save As* from the **FILE** menu and choose any folder on your computer.

Option Two: Installing Templates into *Microsoft Office for Windows*

Installing templates into *Microsoft Office* allows one easy access to templates without inserting the CD-ROM each time.

To install all of the templates, complete the following steps:

1. Create a folder called *Teacher Templates* in the *Template* folder located in the *Microsoft Office* folder. To do this, double-click My Computer, then C: drive, then Program Files folder, then the *Microsoft Office* folder and finally the Templates folder. Choose *New Folder* from the **FILE** menu on the Templates folder menu bar. Name this folder Teacher Templates. Note: If you installed *Microsoft Office* in a different directory locate your files and follow the same steps.

Windows screen

2. Double-click the My Computer icon, then the CD-ROM drive.
3. Choose *Select All* from the **EDIT** menu of the Window.
4. When all of the files have been highlighted, select Copy from the **EDIT** menu.
5. Locate the Teacher Templates folder that you created in step one and open it. Do this by double-clicking My Computer icon, then the C: drive icon, then the Program Files folder, then Microsoft Office folder, then the Templates folder, and finally the Teacher Template folder.
6. Select *Paste* from the **EDIT** menu.

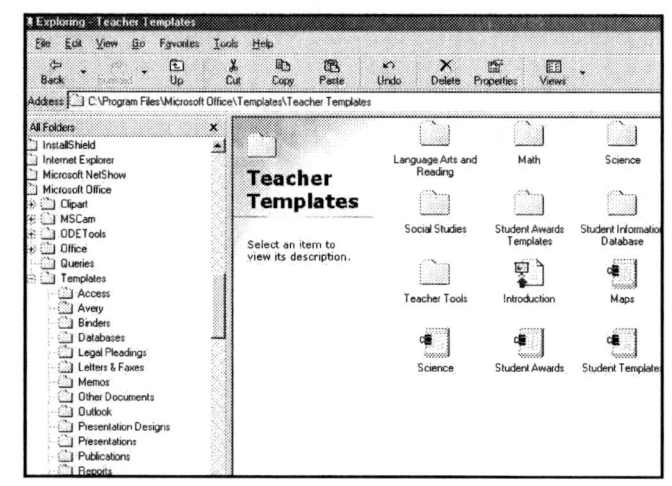

You can now use all of the templates in *Microsoft Office* by selecting *New* in the **FILE** menu in any *Microsoft Office* component (*Word, Excel, PowerPoint,* and *Access*) and opening the Teacher Template folder.

Installing and Using Templates with a Macintosh

There are two options with which to use these templates on your computer.

Option One: Opening Templates from the CD-ROM

The easiest way to use this collection is to open the templates directly from the CD-ROM. The drawback to this method is that you must insert the CD-ROM whenever you wish to use a template. To open templates directly from the CD-ROM, complete the following steps:

1. Double-click the CD-ROM icon located on the desktop.
2. Select the file you wish to use and double-click it.
3. To save any of your changes simply select *Save As* from the **FILE** menu and choose any folder on your computer.

Option Two: Installing Templates into *Microsoft Office* for the Macintosh

1. Create a folder called *Teacher Templates* in the *Template* folder located in the *Microsoft Office* folder. To do this, locate the *Microsoft Office* folder on your Macintosh HD and double-click it to open. Then double-click the Templates folder. Create a new folder by choosing *New Folder* from the **FILE** menu. Name the folder Teacher Templates.
2. Open the CD-ROM and choose *Select All* from the **EDIT** menu.
3. Click and drag the files to the Teacher Template folder that you created in the *Microsoft Office* Template folder.

You can now use all of the templates in *Microsoft Office* by selecting *New* in the **FILE** menu in any *Microsoft Office* component (*Word, Excel,* and *PowerPoint*) and opening the Teacher Template folder.

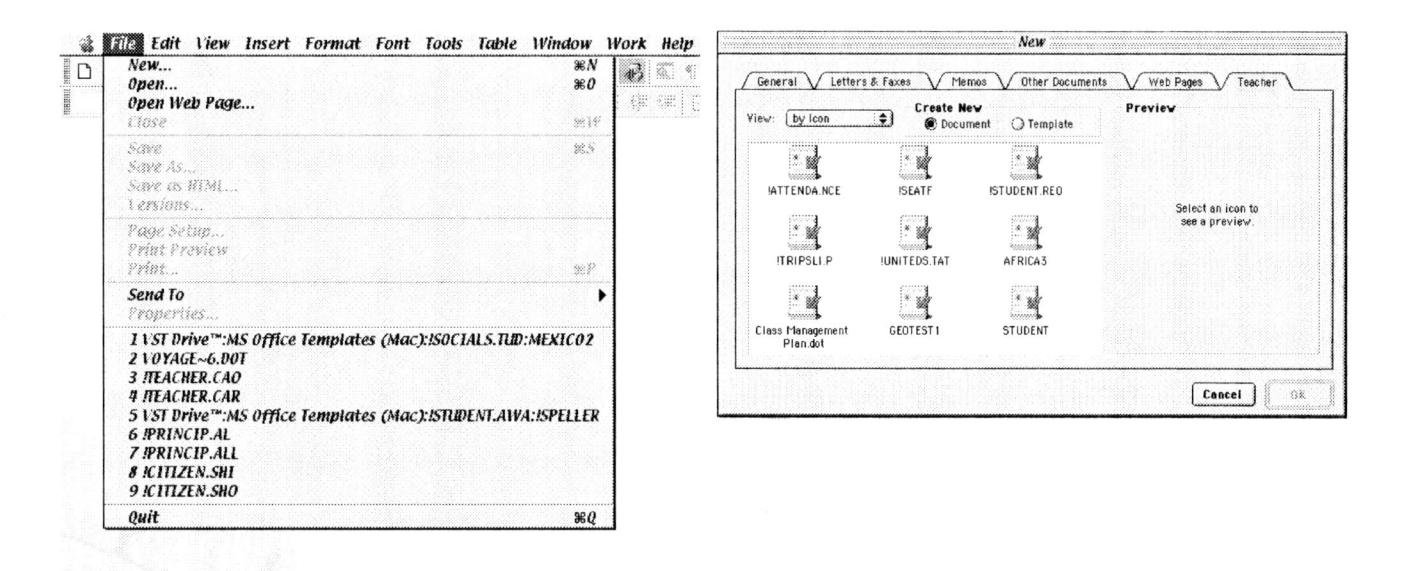

© Teacher Created Resources, Inc. #2771 Teachers' Template Collection for Microsoft Office

Teacher Templates for Microsoft Word

The *Microsoft Word* templates cover a variety of tasks teacher do everyday. These templates offer teachers an assortment of class management screens designed to assist them in carrying out their day-to-day tasks. Template screens include seating charts, awards, letters to parents, permission slips, class inventory lists, and much more.

The entire collection of templates can be used as a series of portfolio exhibits that can show growth in writing and math skills over time.

This template collection also supports teaching across the curriculum. Teachers have access to templates designed with the purpose of building a bridge for students by having them write across the curriculum using the *Storybook Maker* template using *Microsoft Word*. These templates can be printed out and photocopied, or you can allow a student to complete the assignment on the computer.

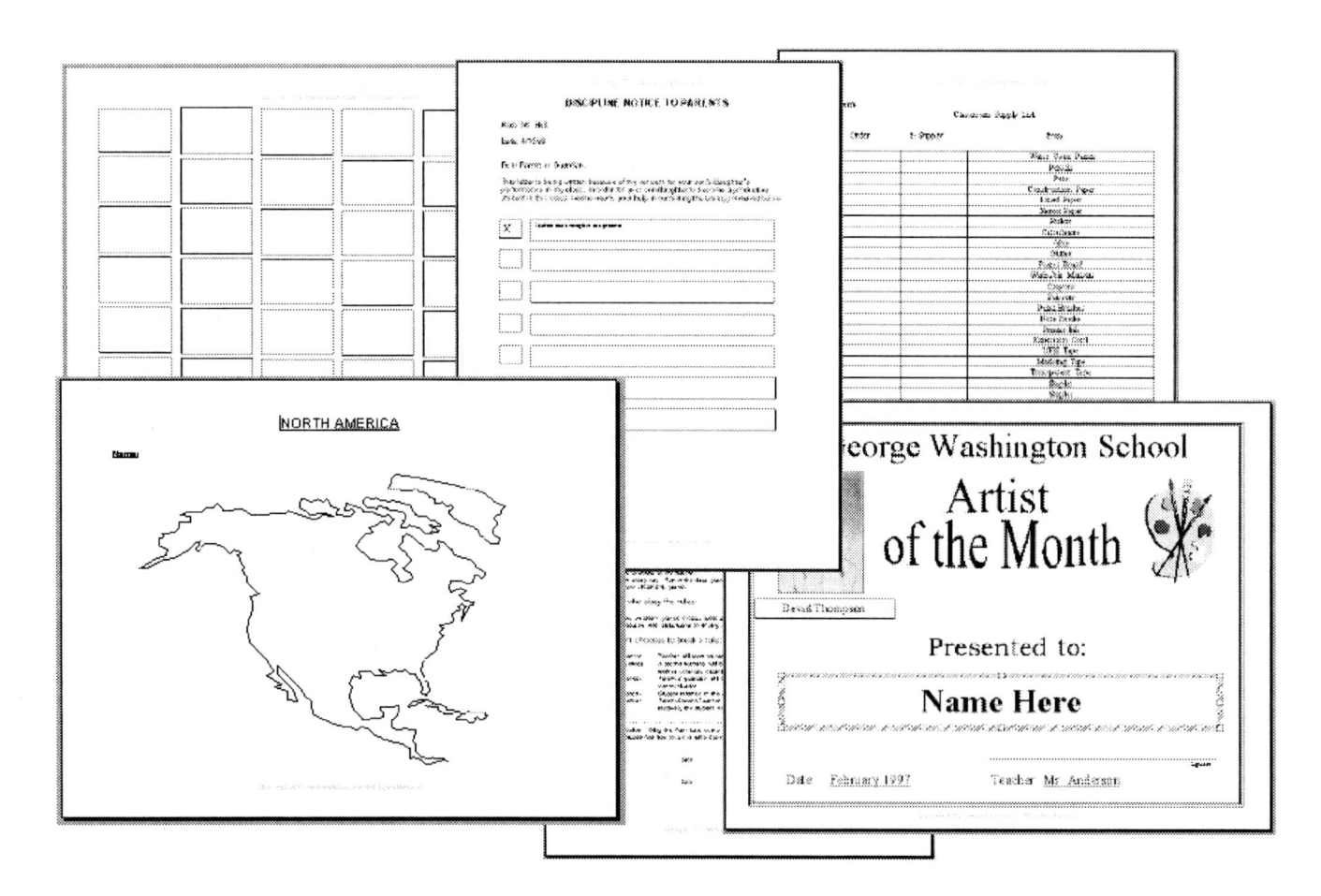

Teacher Templates for Microsoft Word

Seating Charts

This template collection provides eight different seating charts to assist teachers with different classroom arrangements in order to organize students' seating assignments. These charts are in black and white, but some of them on the CD-ROM are in color. All of the templates operate in the same manner. To enter a student's name, click the box that represents a student's seat to highlight it. Type the name of the student in that seat into the box, and repeating the same process for each box.

You can alter a template by doing the following:

1. Increase or decrease the text size and color by using the text options in the **Text** menu (Windows) or **FONT** menu (Macintosh).

2. Add or delete student desks by clicking a student seat box to highlight it, then either use the **Copy** and **Paste** features on the **EDIT** menu to add student desks or **Delete** the highlighted box to remove student desks.

3. Rearrange the student desks by clicking on the student box and holding the right mouse button (Windows) or mouse button (Macintosh) to drag the box to the desired location.

4. To add color to the student box or text, highlight the student box and select the **Fill Color** button on the **Drawing** tool bar.

Note: Some seating charts are grouped. To ungroup, open the **Drawing** tool bar, click the **Draw** button from the tool bar, and select **Ungroup**. There are two additional seating chart templates in the *Microsoft Excel* section.

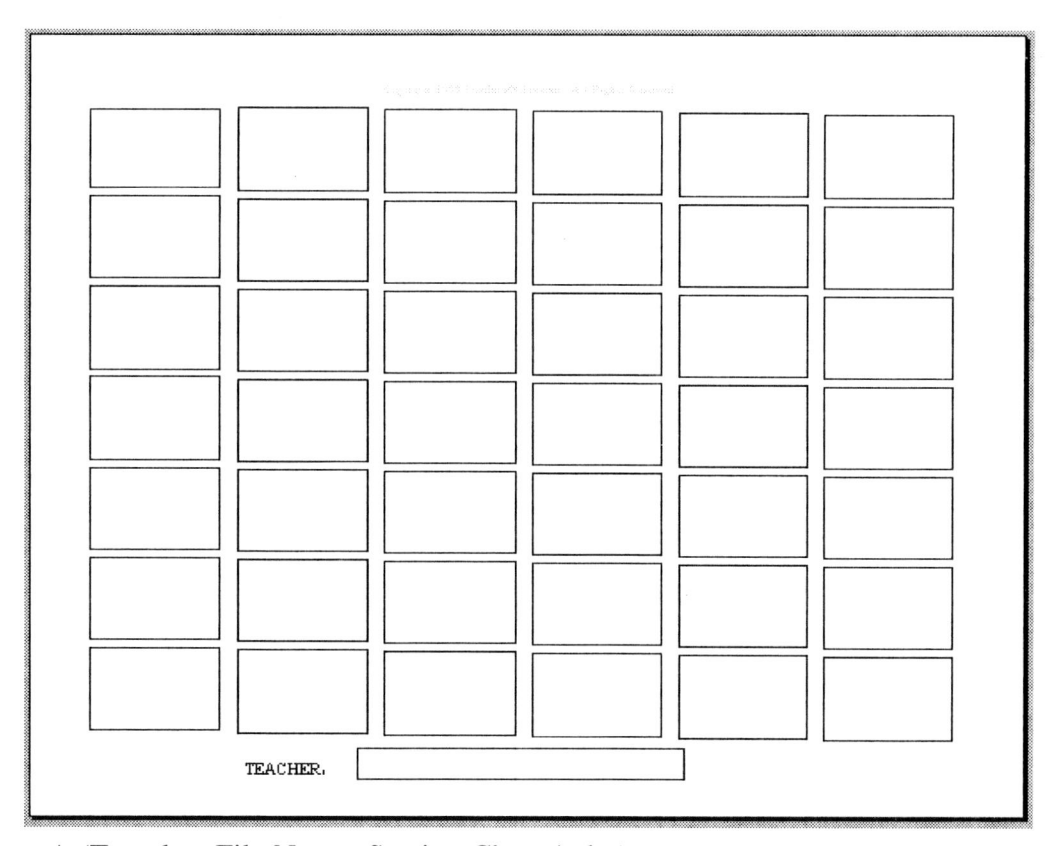

Seating Chart A (Template File Name: Seating Chart A.dot)

© *Teacher Created Resources, Inc.*

Teacher Templates for Microsoft Word

Seating Charts *(cont.)*

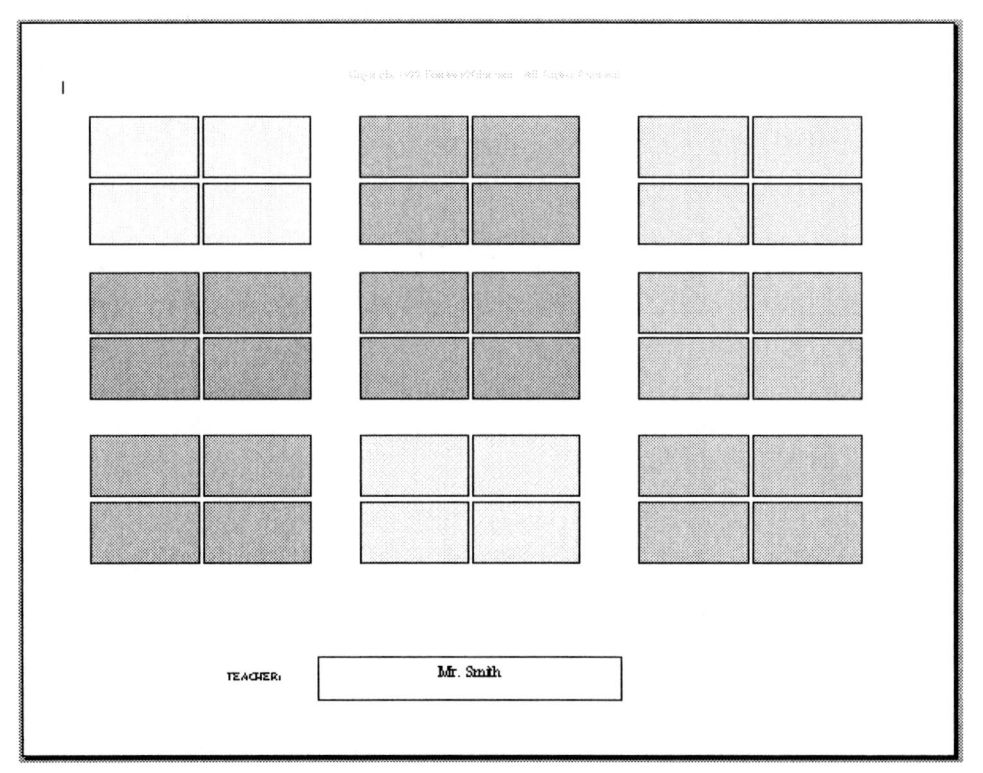

Seating Chart B (Template File Name: Seating Chart B.dot)

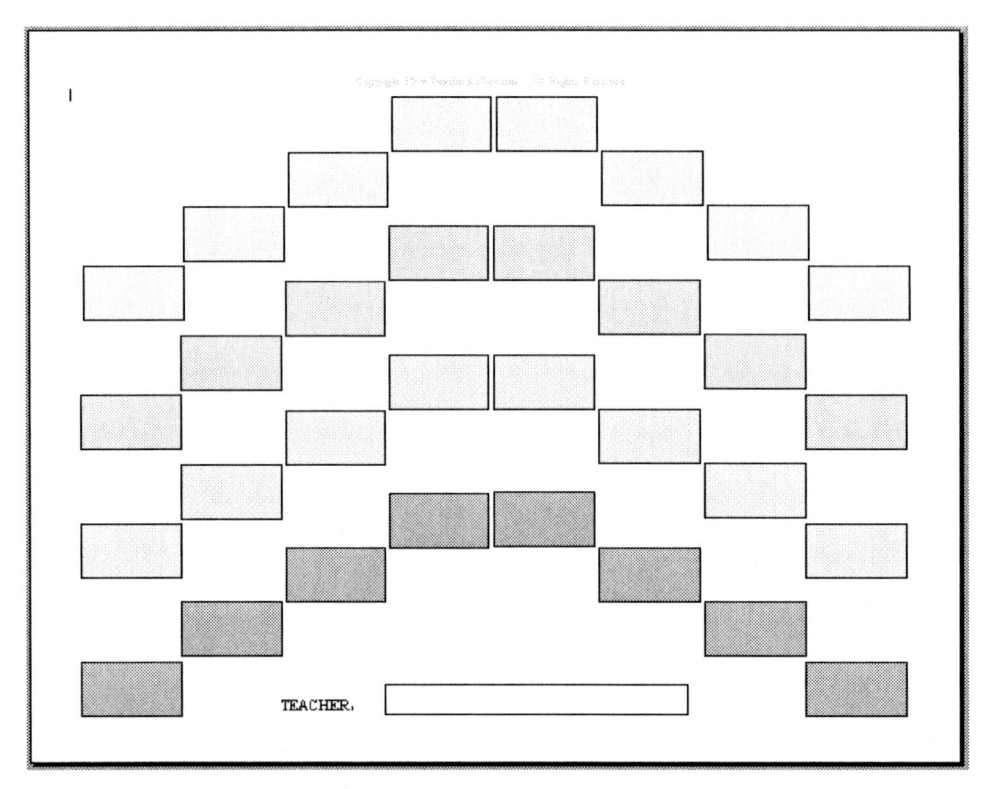

Seating Chart C (Template File Name: Seating Chart C.dot)

Teacher Templates for Microsoft Word

Seating Charts *(cont.)*

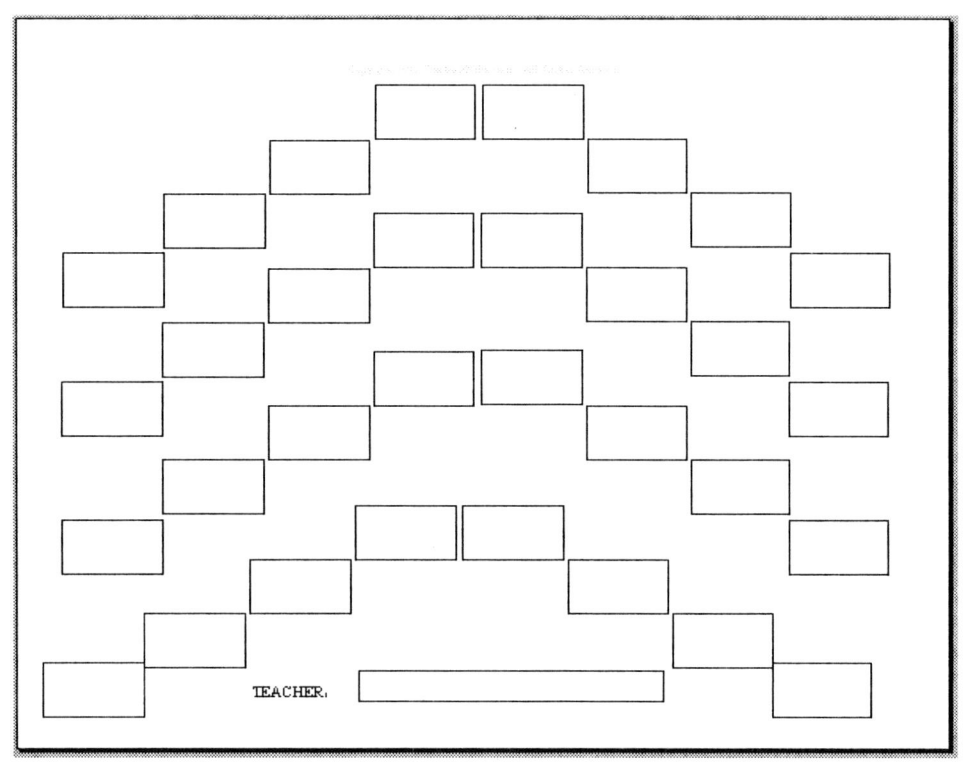

Seating Chart D (Template File Name: Seating Chart D.dot)

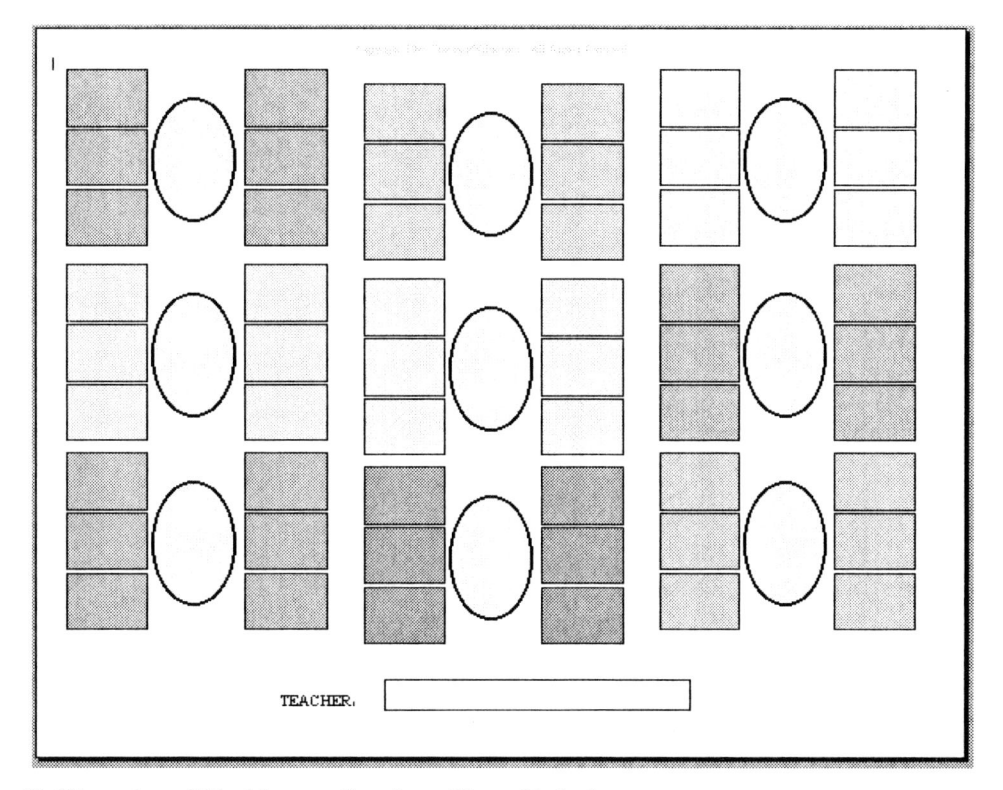

Seating Chart E (Template File Name: Seating Chart E.dot)

© *Teacher Created Resources, Inc.* 11 #2771 *Teachers' Template Collection for Microsoft Office*

Teacher Templates for Microsoft Word

Seating Charts *(cont.)*

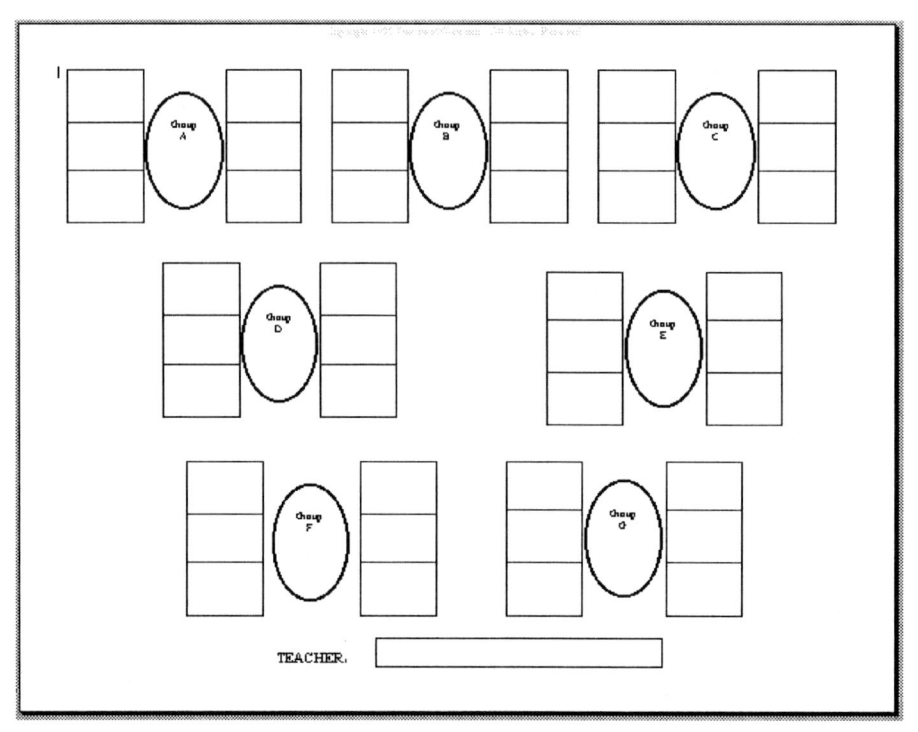

Seating Chart F (Template File Name: Seating Chart F.dot)

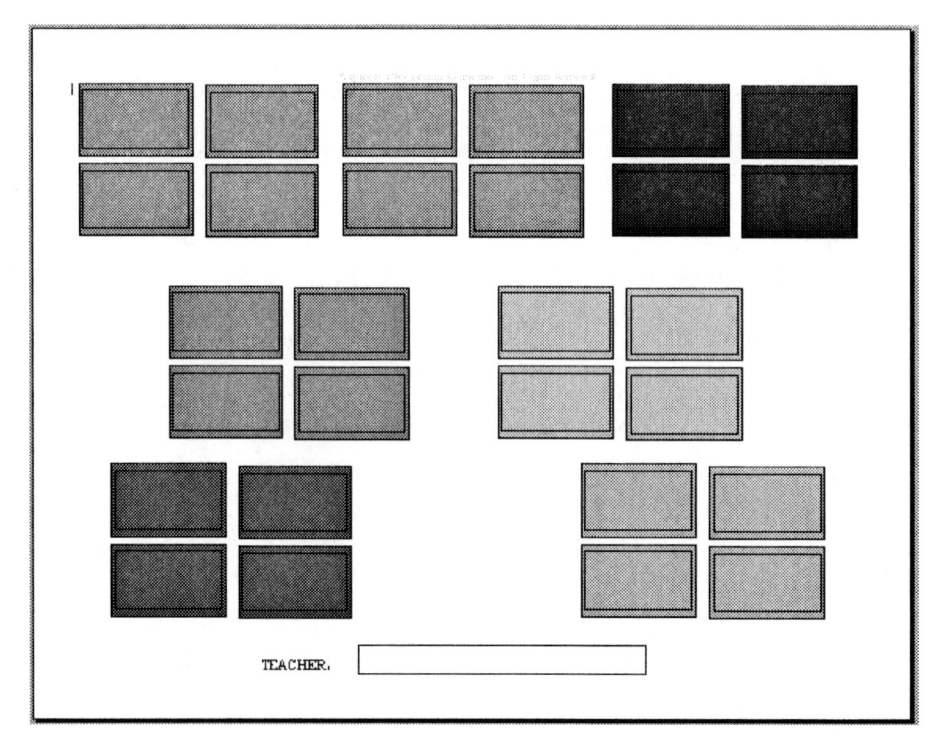

Seating Chart G (Template File Name: Seating Chart G.dot)

The CD-ROM contains one other seating chart not pictured here.(Template File Name: Seating Chart H.dot)

Teacher Templates for Microsoft Word

Student Awards

The Student Awards templates contain a collection of awards teachers can use to highlight student achievement and merit.

To edit the templates follow these simple steps.

1. To change a student's picture, the picture to be inserted should already have been scanned or loaded as a file on a disk or the hard drive. Double-click the picture in the award, and you will enter the *Microsoft Photo Gallery*. Find the new picture on your computer to insert by clicking the Import button. After you have located the image, click Insert. You may have to resize or move the image once it is pasted onto your award document. See your manual about importing and resizing pictures for *Microsoft Office*.

2. To change the title of the award, double-click on the title, and you will go to the *WordArt Gallery* screen. Enter the name of the award. You can also change and edit the size, color, and style of the text.

3. To change the name of the student and the date, click the name box and enter the name of the student and the date.

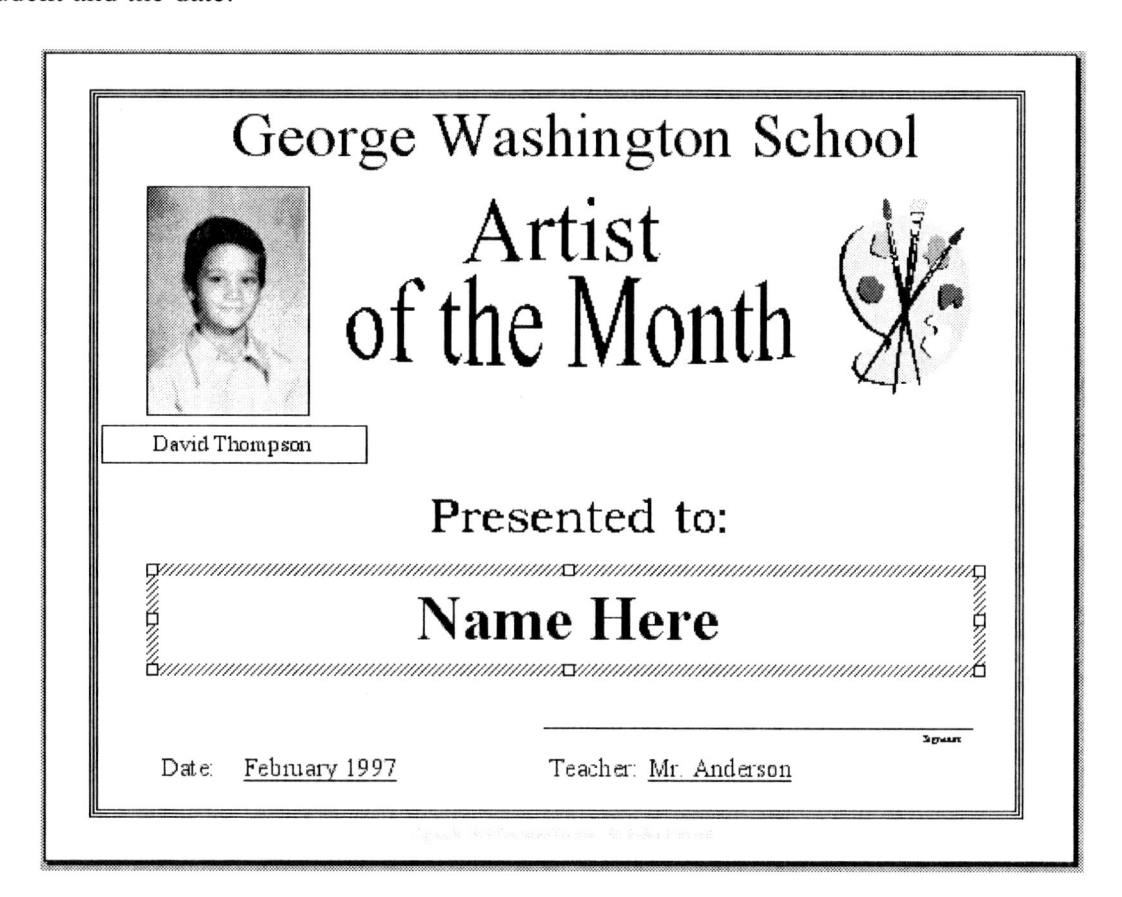

Artist of the Month (Template File Name: Artist of the Month(L).dot)

A second Artist of the Month certificate which is laid out in portrait orientation is available on the CD-ROM. (Template File Name: Artist of the Month.dot)

Teacher Templates for Microsoft Word

Student Awards *(cont.)*

Perfect Attendance (Template File Name: Perfect Attendance.dot)

Perfect Attendance Landscape (Template File Name: Perfect Attendance(L).dot)

Teacher Templates for Microsoft Word

Student Awards *(cont.)*

Library Helper (Template File Name: Library Helper.dot)

Library Helper Landscape (Template File Name: Library Helper.dot)

© *Teacher Created Resources, Inc.* 15 #2771 *Teachers' Template Collection for Microsoft Office*

Teacher Templates for Microsoft Word

Student Awards *(cont.)*

Book Monitor of the Month (Template File Name: Book Monitor(L).dot)

Book Monitor of the Month (Template File Name: Book Monitor.dot)

Athlete of the Month Landscape (Template File Name: Athlete of the Month(L).dot)

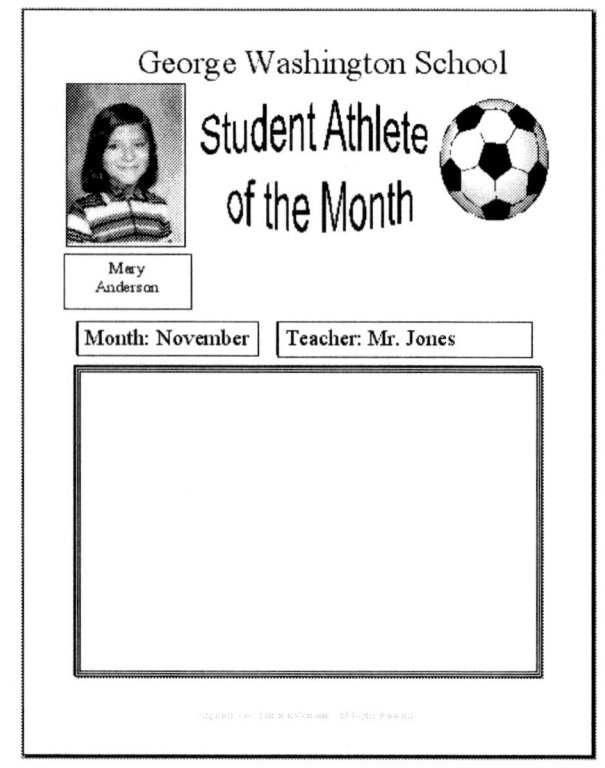

Athlete of the Month (Template File Name: Athlete of the Month.dot)

Student Awards *(cont.)*

Citizenship Award Month (Template File Name: Citizenship(L).dot)

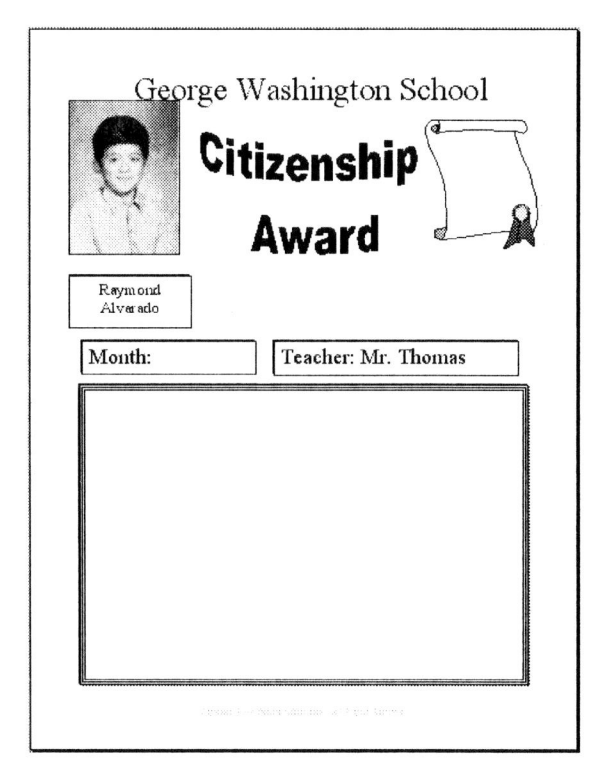

Citizenship Award Month (Template File Name: Citizenship.dot)

Student of the Month Landscape (Template File Name: Student of the Month(L).dot)

Student of the Month Landscape (Template File Name: Student of the Month.dot)

Teacher Templates for Microsoft Word

Student Awards *(cont.)*

Principal's Student of the Month Landscape(Template File Name: Principal's Student of the Month(L).dot)

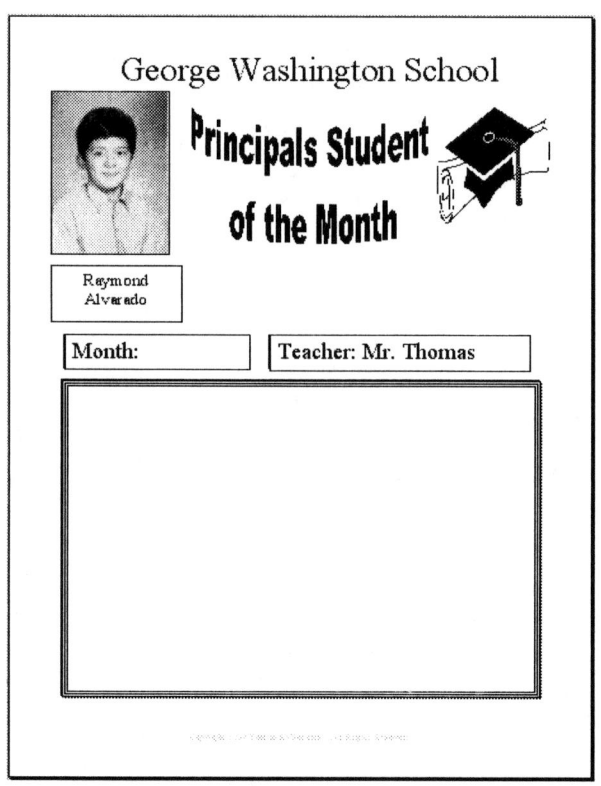

Principal's Student of the Month (Template File Name: Principal's Student of the Month.dot)

Speller of the Month Landscape (Template File Name: Speller of the Month(L).dot)

Speller of the Month (Template File Name: Speller of the Month.dot)

Student Awards *(cont.)*

Student Helper of the Month (Template File Name: Student Helper of the Month.dot)

Student Helper of the Month Landscape (Template File Name: Student Helper of the Month(L).dot)

Teacher Templates for Microsoft Word

Student Awards *(cont.)*

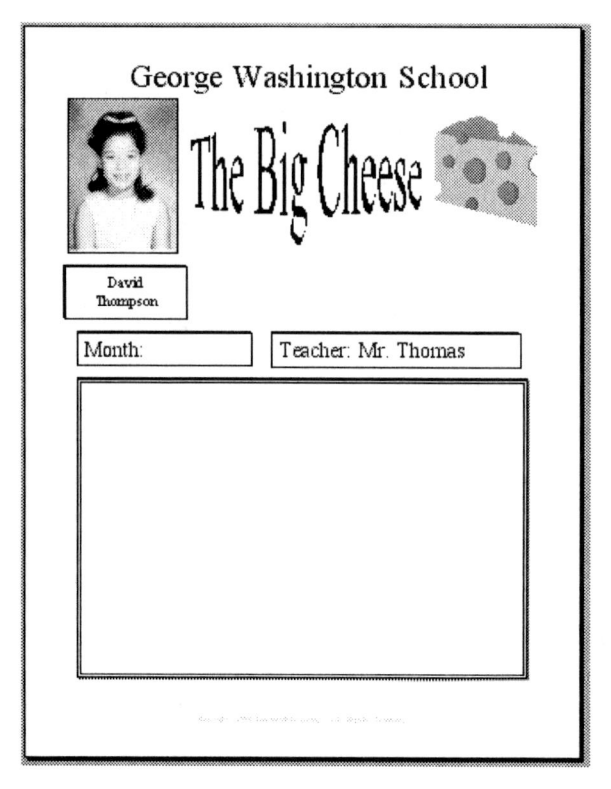

The Big Cheese (Template File Name: The Big Cheese.dot)

The Big Cheese Landscape(Template File Name: The Big Cheese(L).dot)

Teacher Templates for Microsoft Word

Teacher Documents

This section contains a collection of teacher document templates that will be of use to all teachers across all grade levels. They are documents that can be useed by the teachers for the day-to-day activities in the classroom. They include:

- Letters home
- Class management plan
- Lesson plan
- Notes for substitute
- Classroom inventory sheet
- Teacher business card
- School trip slip
- Memo slip
- Discipline notice

To edit any of these documents, click the section within the document you wish to change and type in your changes. To modify the Header or Footer, click that area of the document, and the header or footer section will become activated. This is the area that contains the name of your school. Highlight and delete any text you do not want and enter your information.

Classroom Inventory Sheet (Template File Name: Classroom Inventory.dot)

Teacher Templates for Microsoft Word

Teacher Documents (cont.)

George Washington School

Student Name [ ]   Date [ ]

Classroom Management Plan

Teacher Name: Janice Underwood

The goal of this class is to learn about an aspect of business that will help you to have the skills and knowledge necessary for life. Learning something new requires your best effort. The following rules will help you give your best effort.

Students are expected to:

1. Be in their seats and ready to work when the tardy bell rings.
2. Bring to class materials needed to complete the daily assignments.
3. Use time wisely by working on the current assignment until completed. Use extra time for working ahead, making up work, and/or doing assignments for other classes.
4. Work independently and quietly, have a positive attitude, and be polite to all people.
5. Raise hand for help when needed then wait patiently and quietly until the teacher can help.
6. NO PASSES. Take care of going to the restroom and drinking fountain before coming to class.
7. NO FOOD, DRINK, or GUM should be brought into the room. During candy sales, the candy should be left with the teacher until class is over.
8. Take care of the equipment and books provided for completing your work. Report any damage to the equipment or books to the teacher.
9. Be present every day. Part of the class grade is based upon attendance. Also, unexcused absences will lower your citizenship grade.

Students who obey the rules:

1. Will receive excellent grades in class work and citizenship.
2. Will be prepared with skills useful in finding a job and preparing for future life experiences.

If a student chooses to break a rule:

1st Consequence:	Teacher will warn student that the rule was broken.
2nd Consequence:	A second warning will be given with the possible consequence of after school work or voluntary cleaning.
3rd Consequence:	Parent or guardian will be notified by phone, progress report, or written communication.
4th Consequence:	Student referred to the counselor
5th Consequence:	Parent-Student-Teacher conference with counselor. If the problem cannot be resolved, the student may be referred to an Assistant Principal for discipline.

- -

Please sign below. Bring this form back to the teacher tomorrow. If there are any questions or comments, please feel free to call or write the comments on the back of this form.

Teacher _____ Date _____ Administrator _____ Date _____

Student _____ Date _____ Parent/Guardian _____ Date _____

Copyright 1999 TeachersOffice.com. All Rights Reserved

Classroom Management Plan (Template File Name: Classroom Management.dot)

Teacher Templates for Microsoft Word

Teacher Documents (cont.)

Classroom Supply List (Template File Name: Class Supply List.dot)

Student Permission Slip (Template File Name: Student Trip Slip.dot)

Teacher Templates for Microsoft Word

Teacher Documents (cont.)

School Rules (Template File Name: School Rules.dot)

Discipline Notice to Parents (Template File Name: Discipline Notice.dot)

Teacher Templates for Microsoft Word

Teacher Documents *(cont.)*

Letter Home (Template File Name: Discipline Letter.dot)

Homework Assignments
(Template File Name:
Homework Assignments.dot)

Teacher Templates for Microsoft Word

Teacher Documents *(cont.)*

Letterhead 1 (Template File Name: Letter Head.dot)

Letterhead 2 (Template File Name: Letter Head 2.dot)

Teacher Templates for Microsoft Word

Teacher Documents *(cont.)*

Memo (Template File Name: Memo.dot)

Memo 2 (Template File Name: Memo 2.dot)

There is a third Memo template on the CD-ROM titled Memo 3.dot.

© Teacher Created Resources, Inc. 27 #2771 Teachers' Template Collection for Microsoft Office

Teacher Templates for Microsoft Word

Teacher Documents *(cont.)*

Teacher Business Cards: (Template File Name: Teacher Cards.dot)

Teacher Business Cards 1: (Template File Name: Teacher Cards1.dot)

There is a third Teacher Business Cards template on the CD-ROM titled Teacher Cards2.dot.

Teacher Templates for Microsoft Word

Teacher Documents *(cont.)*

Notice for Substitute (Template File Name: Notes for Substitute.dot)

Ideas for the Substitute (Template File Name: Ideas for Substitute.dot)

Teacher Templates for Microsoft Word

Teacher Documents *(cont.)*

Week at a Glance

Name: Bill Jones

Science
Key Topic/Goal for the Week

Reading Homework

Math
Key Topic/Goal for the Week

Reading Homework

Reading/Language Arts
Key Topic/Goal for the Week

Reading Homework

Social Science
Key Topic/Goal for the Week

Reading Homework

Health
Key Topic/Goal for the Week

Reading Homework

Week at a Glance (Template File Name: Week at a Glance.dot)

Teacher Templates for Microsoft Word

Maps

The Map templates contain a collection of maps that teachers can use to help students learn geography and topography skills. You may choose to print the map from the template or use the drawing tools to add cities, legends, and note fields to the map document. In addition to the maps pictured below and on the following pages, you will find two geography tests with the file names Geotest 1.dot and Geotest 2.dot.

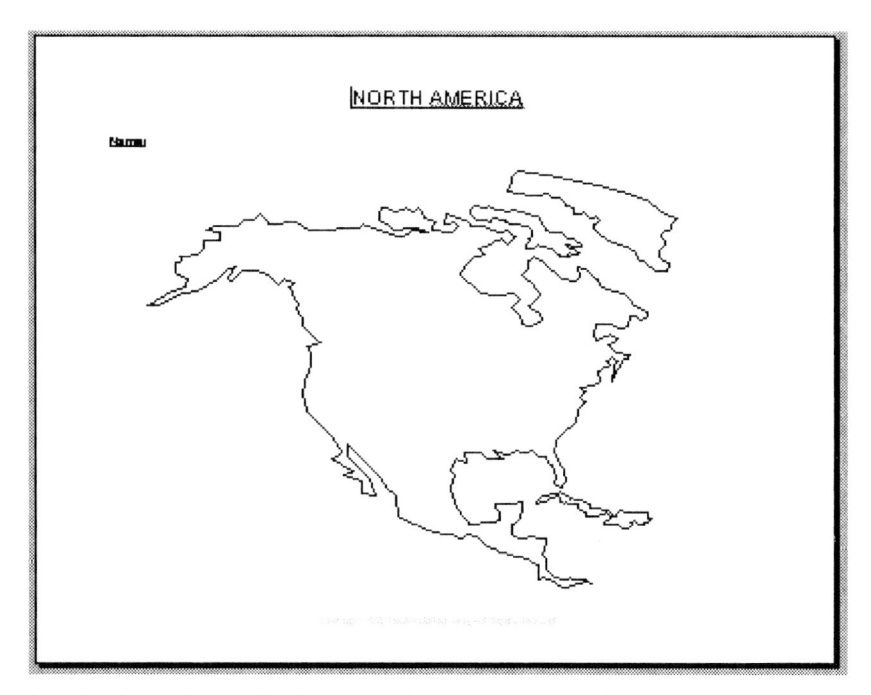

Map of North America 1 (Template File Name: North America Map 1.dot)

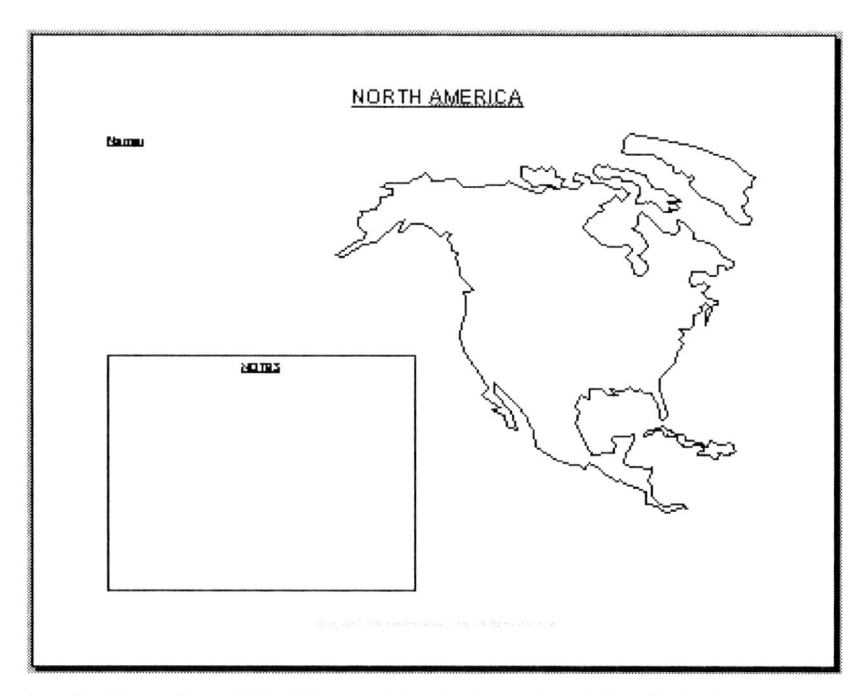

Map of North America 2 (Template File Name: North America Map 2.dot)

© Teacher Created Resources, Inc.

Teacher Templates for Microsoft Word

Maps *(cont.)*

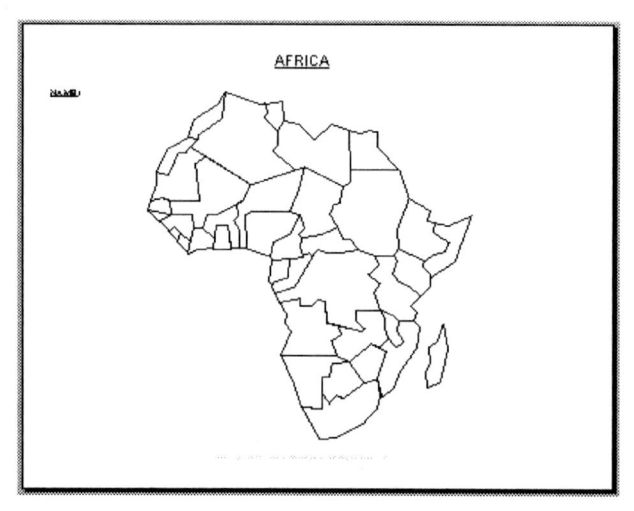

Map of Africa 1 (Template File Name: Africa Map 1.dot)

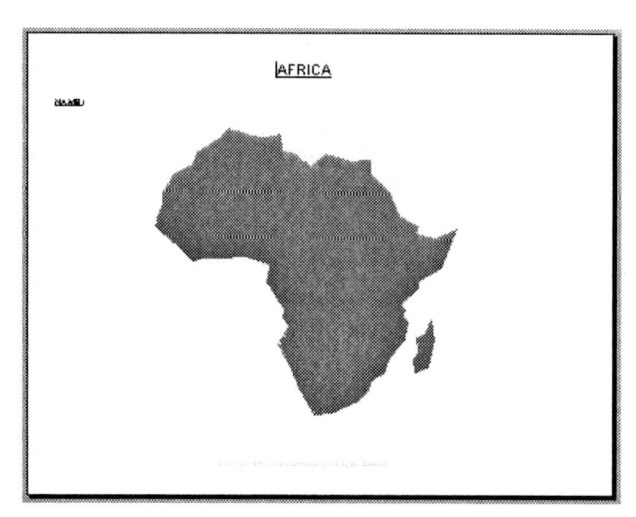

Map of Africa 2 (Template File Name: Africa Map 2.dot)

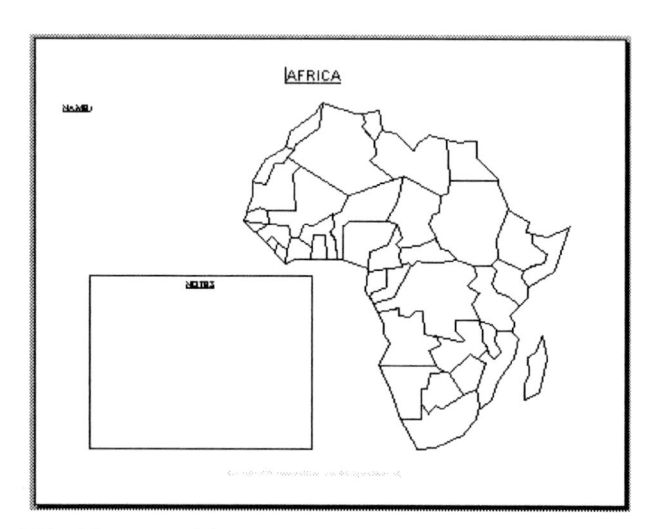

Map of Africa 3 (Template File Name: Africa Map 3.dot)

Teacher Templates for Microsoft Word

Maps *(cont.)*

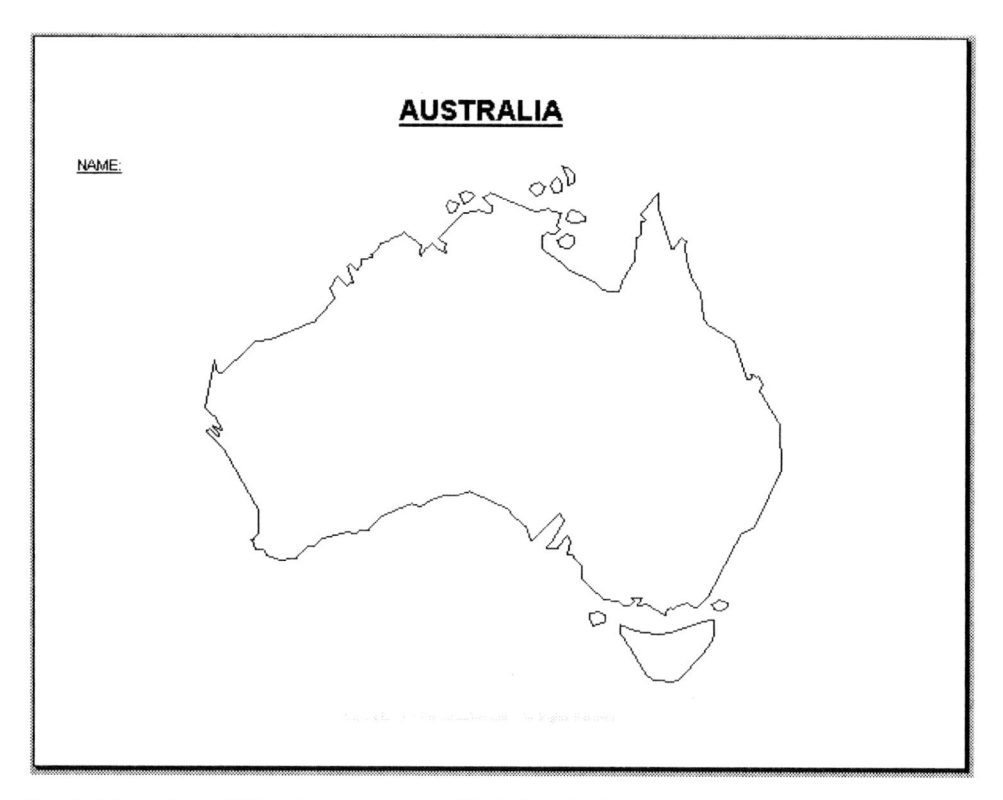

Map of Australia 1 (Template File Name: Australia Map 1.dot)

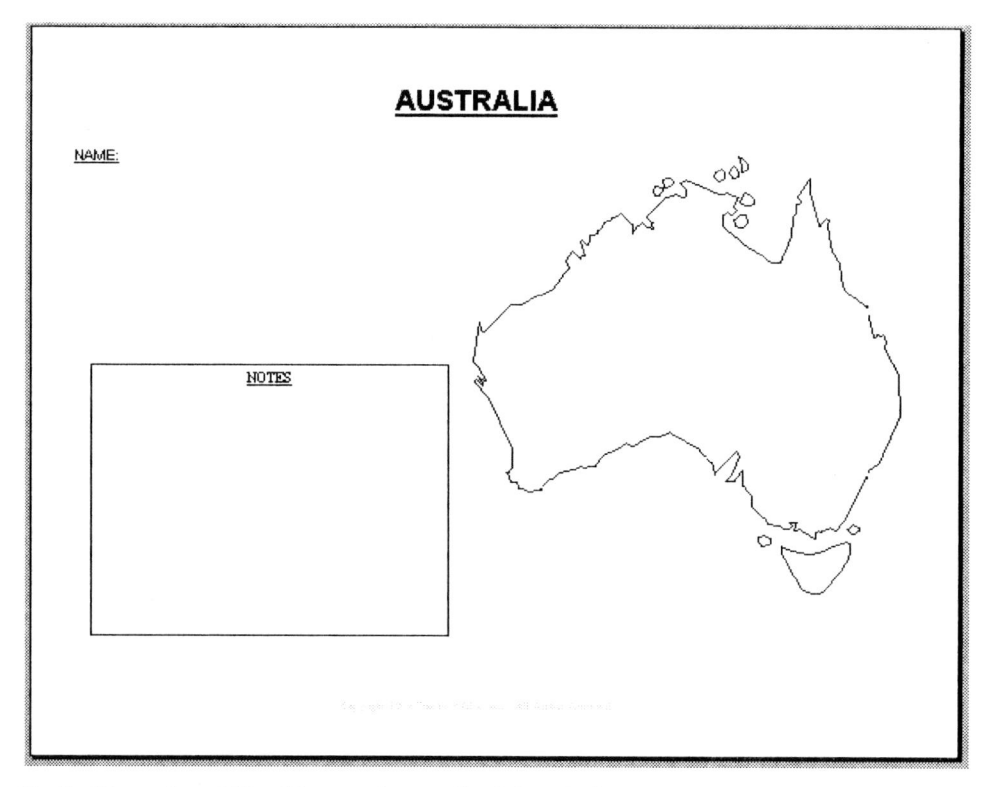

Map of Australia 2 (Template File Name: Australia Map 2.dot)

Teacher Templates for Microsoft Word

Maps *(cont.)*

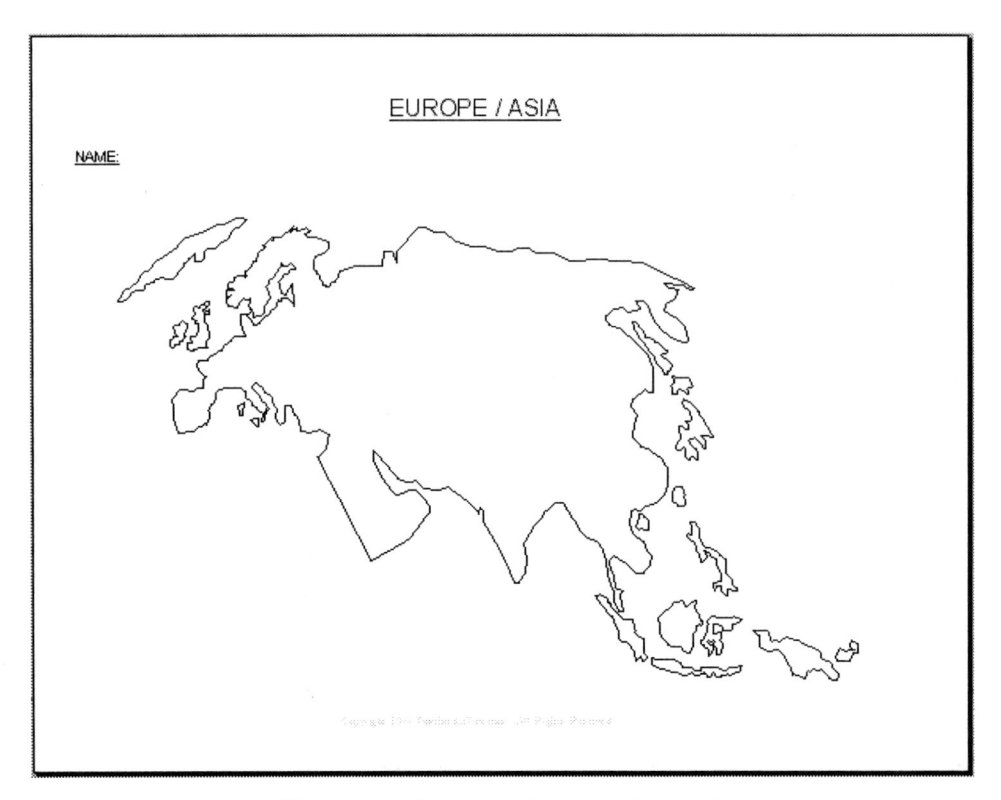

Map of Europe/Asia 1 (Template File Name: Europe & Asia Map 1.dot)

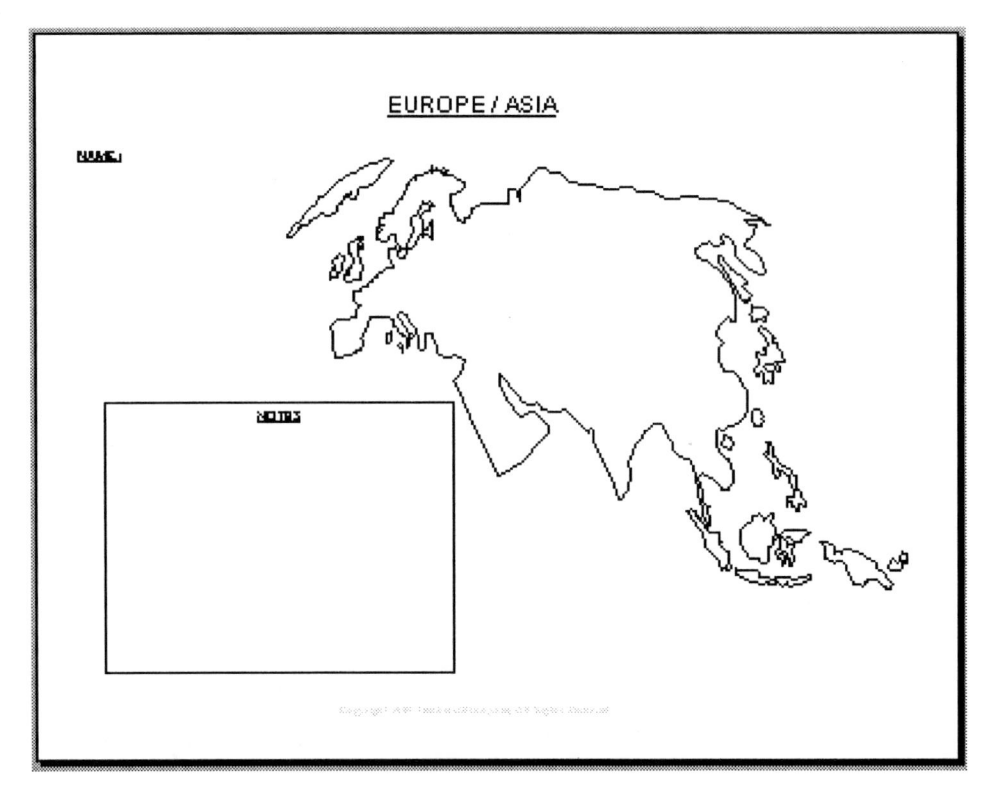

Map of Europe/Asia 2 (Template File Name: Europe & Asia Map 2.dot)

Teacher Templates for Microsoft Word

Maps *(cont.)*

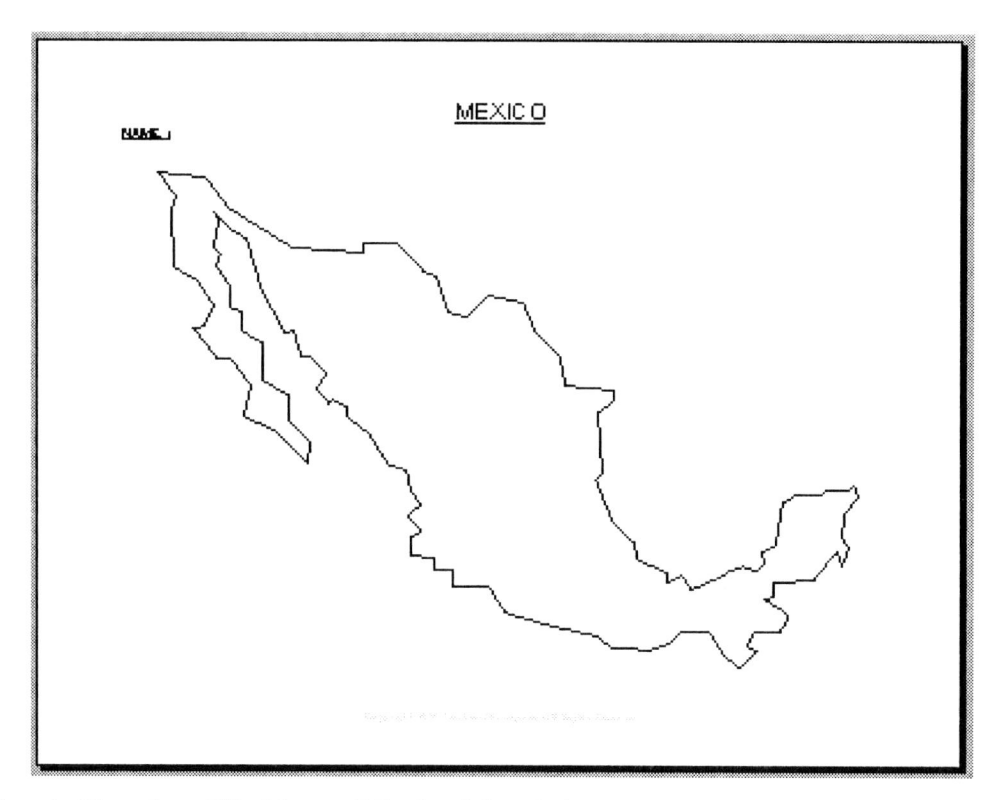

Map of Mexico 1 (Template File Name: Mexico Map 1.dot)

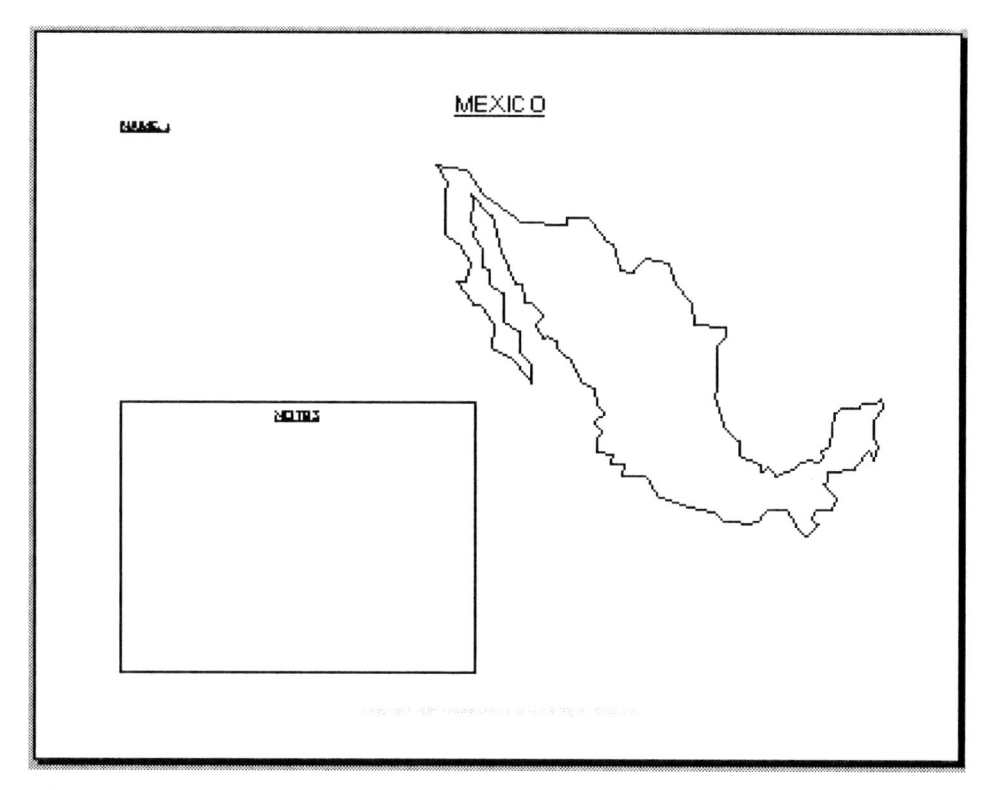

Map of Mexico 2 (Template File Name: Mexico Map 2.dot)

© *Teacher Created Resources, Inc.* #2771 *Teachers' Template Collection for Microsoft Office*

Teacher Templates for Microsoft Word

Maps *(cont.)*

Map of South America 1 (Template File Name: South America Map 1.dot)

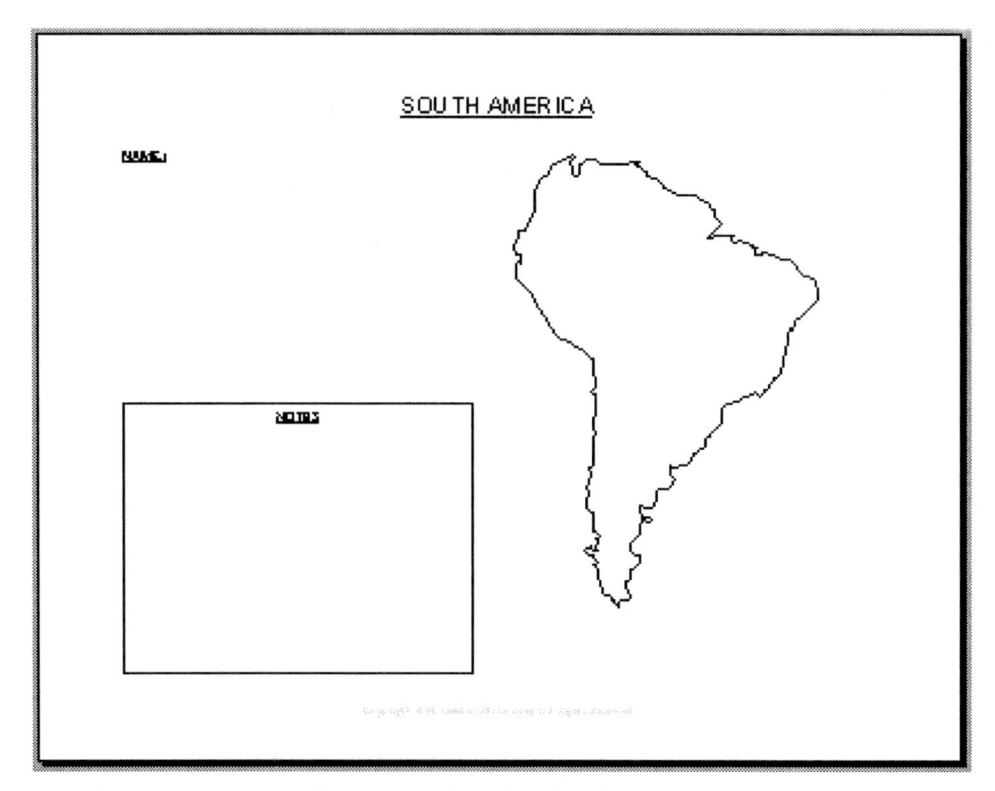

Map of South America 2 (Template File Name: South America Map 2.dot)

Teacher Templates for Microsoft Word

Maps *(cont.)*

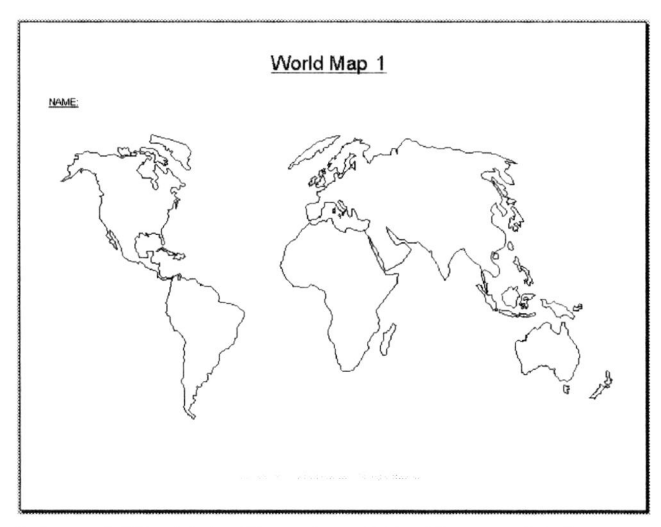

Map of World 1 (Template File Name: Globe Map 1.dot)

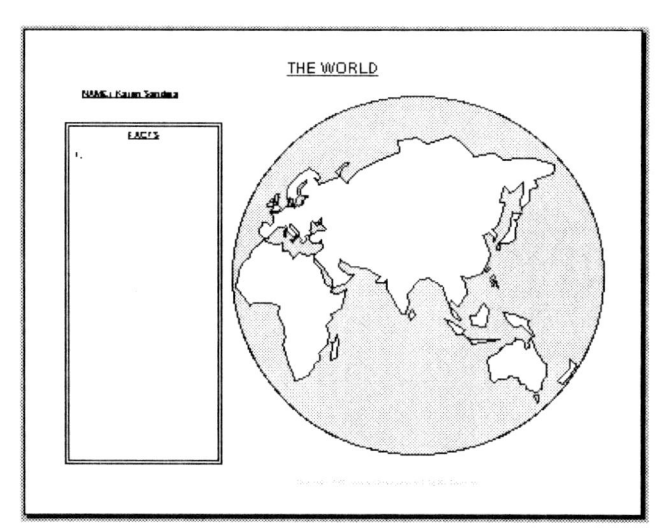

Map of the World 2 (Template File Name: Globe Map 2.dot)

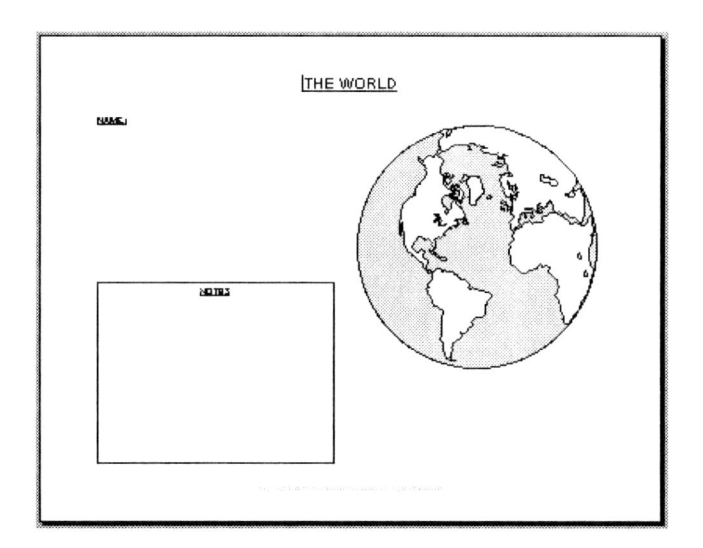

Map of the World 3 (Template File Name: Globe Map 3.dot)

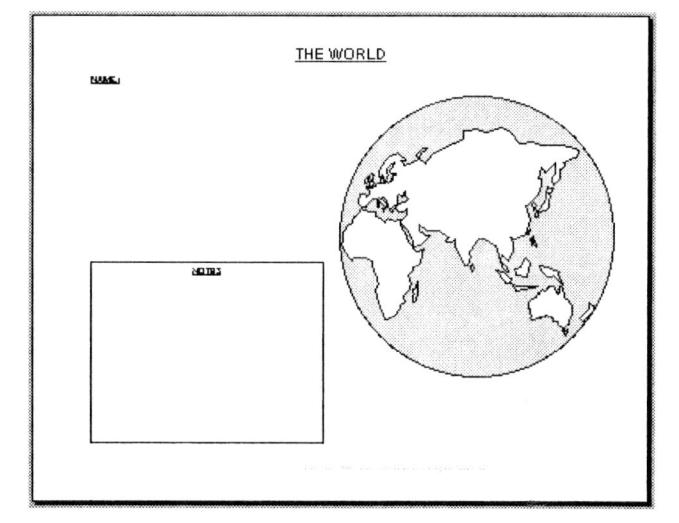

Map of the World 4 (Template File Name: Globe Map 4.dot)

© *Teacher Created Resources, Inc.* 37 *#2771 Teachers' Template Collection for Microsoft Office*

Teacher Templates for Microsoft Word

Maps *(cont.)*

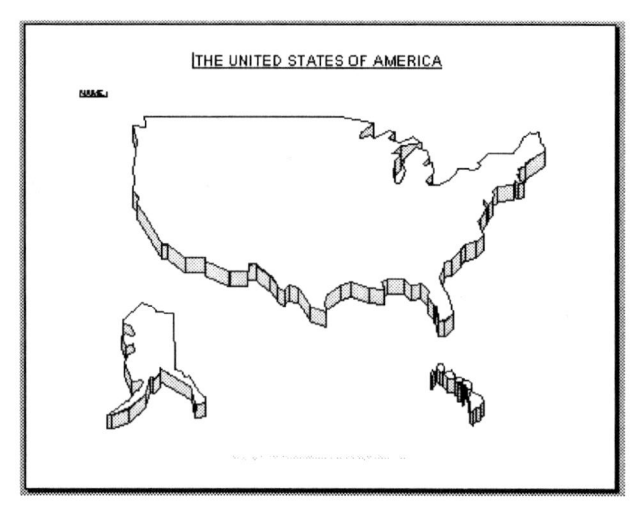

Map of theUnited States 1 (Template File Name: United States Map 1.dot)

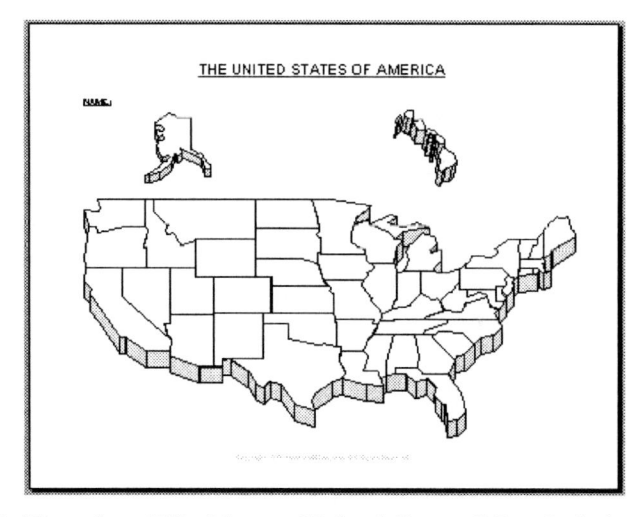

Map of the United States 2 (Template File Name: United States Map 2.dot)

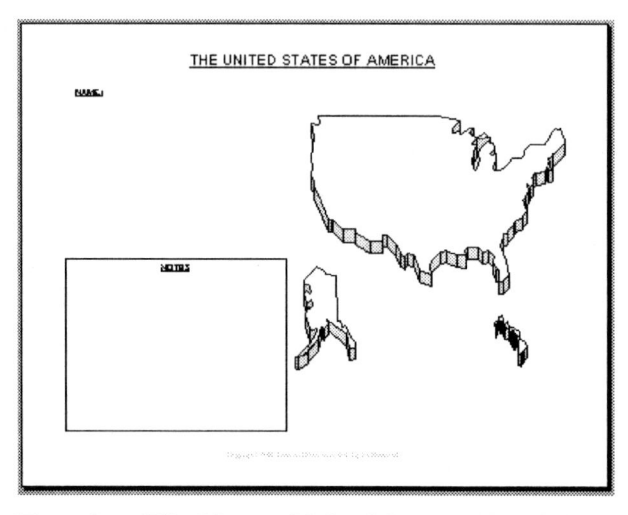

Map of the United States 3 (Template File Name: United States Map 3.dot)

Teacher Templates for Microsoft Word

Voyages to the Past

The Voyages to the Past templates are ideal for expanding the Social Studies curriculum. There is an important need to help students make connections between continents and cultures. Images located in the document will help students recall knowledge they may already have on the subject. Teachers can change the template by replacing the clip art and creating questions or writing topics for students to answer.

To replace the clip art, double-click the image and select a new image from the *Microsoft Clip Gallery* or your own clip art files.

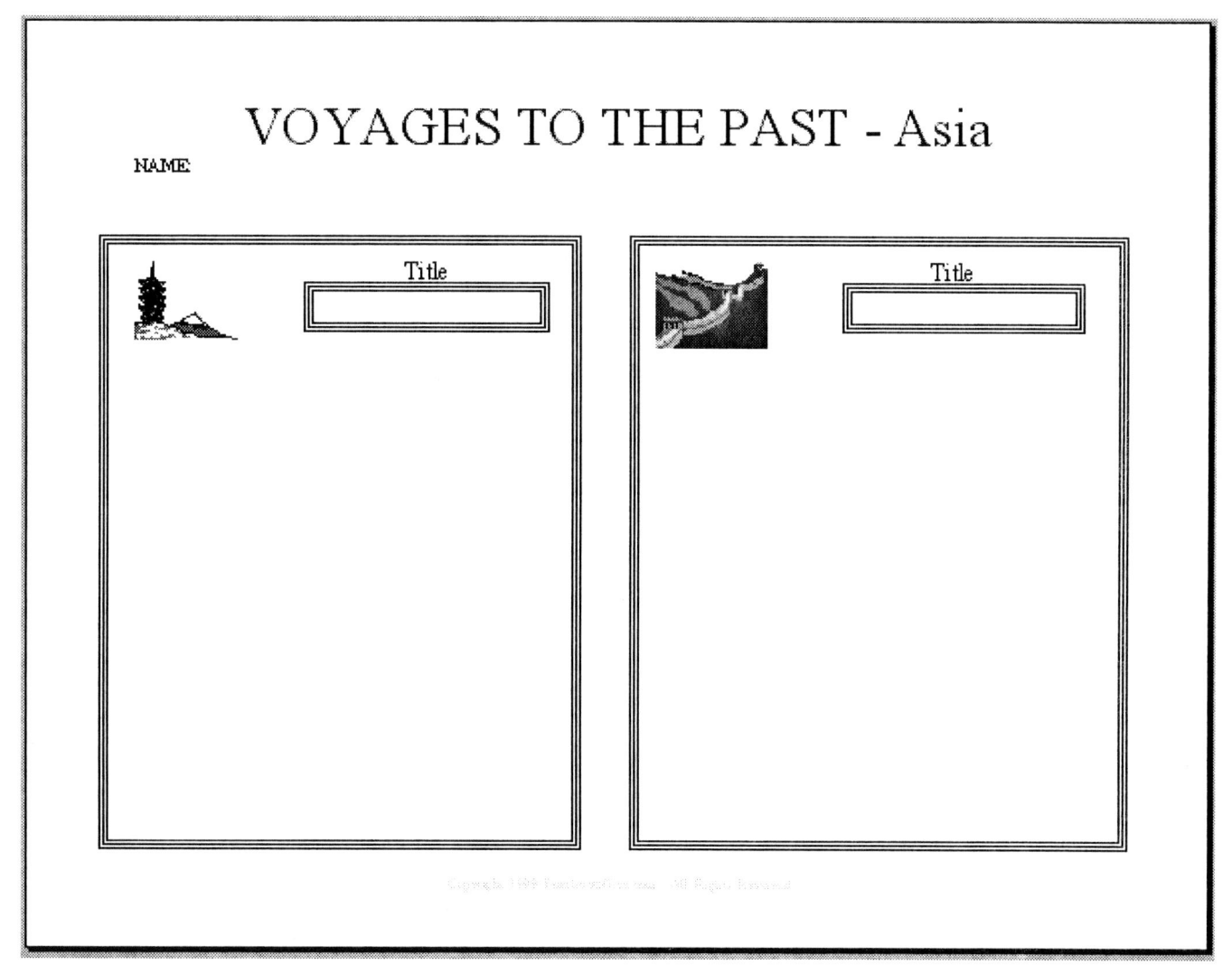

Voyages to the Past—Asia (Template File Name: Voyages to the Past Asia 1.dot)

Teacher Templates for Microsoft Word

Voyages to the Past *(cont.)*

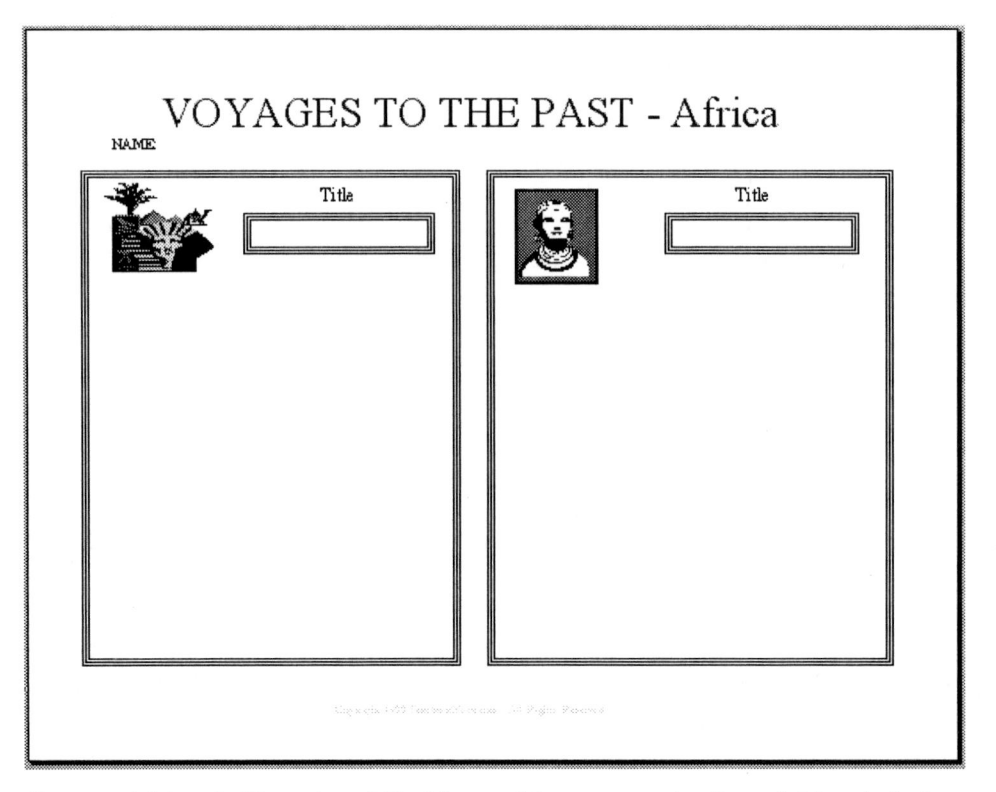

Voyages to the Past —Africa 1 (Template File Name: Voyages to the Past Africa 1.dot)

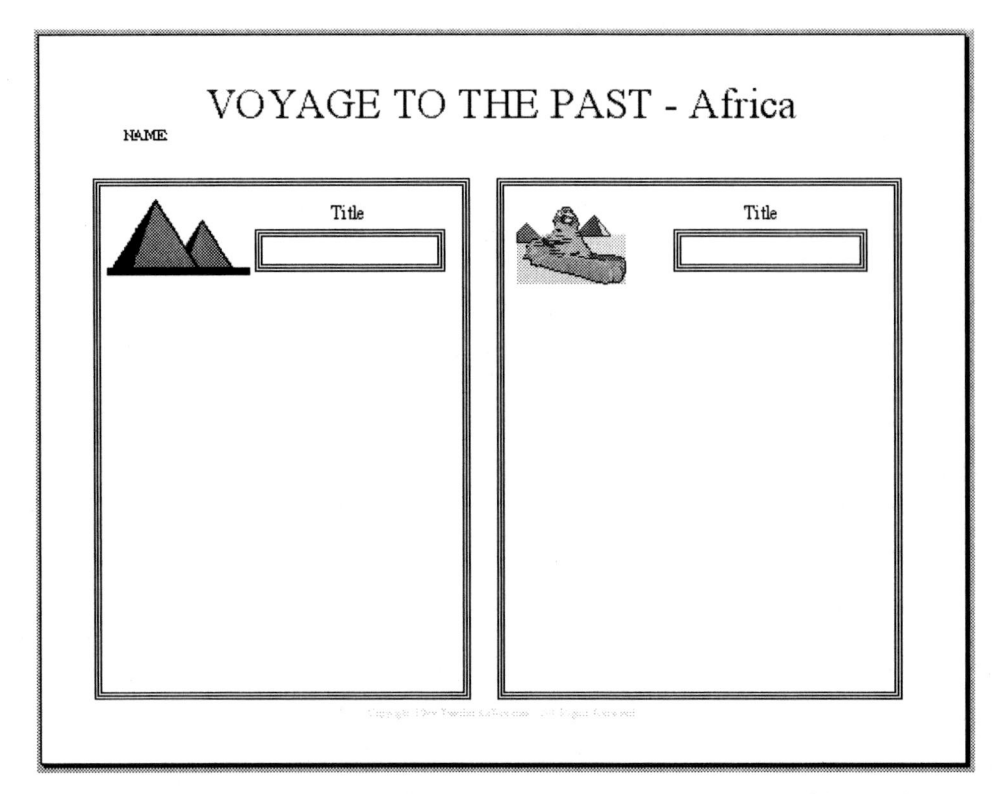

Voyages to the Past —Africa 2 (Template File Name: Voyages to the Past Africa 2.dot)

Teacher Templates for Microsoft Word

Voyages to the Past *(cont.)*

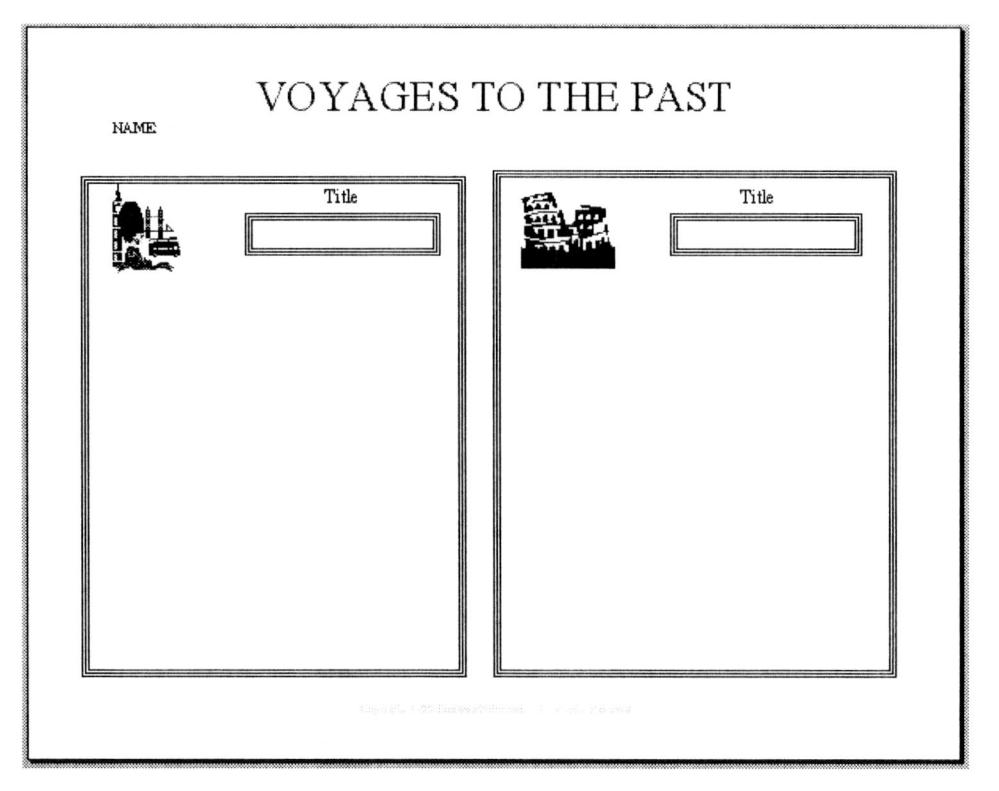

Voyages to the Past—Europe 1 (Template File Name: Voyages to the Past Europe 1.dot)

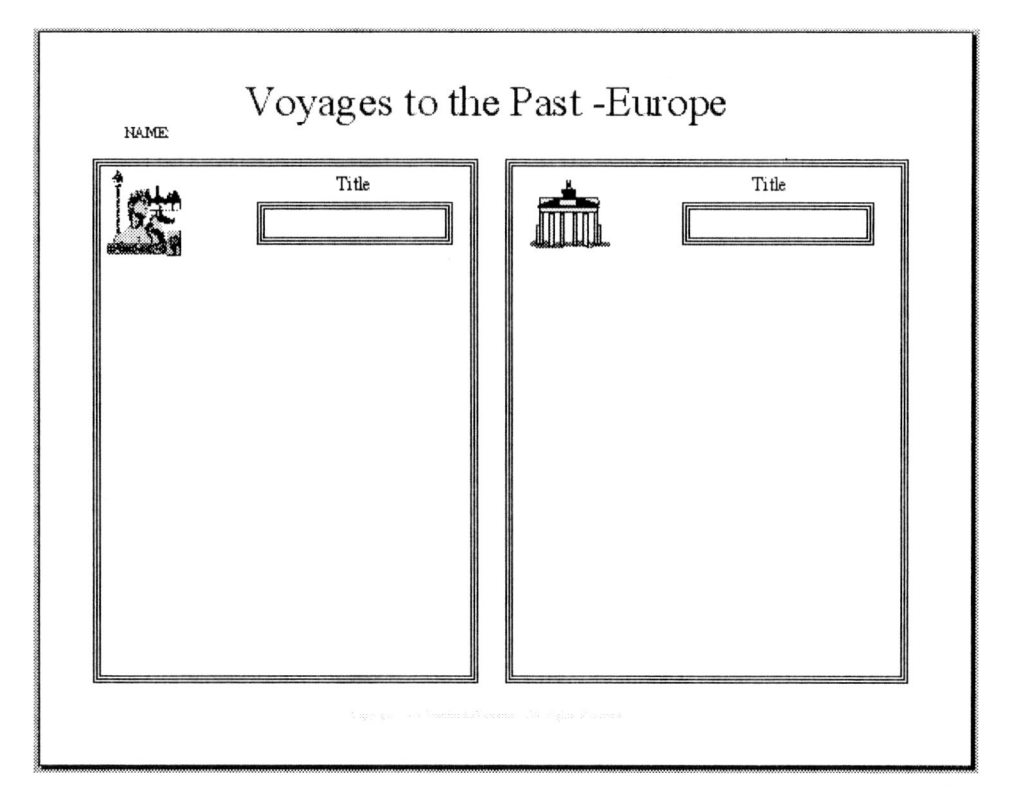

Voyages to the Past—Europe 2 (Template File Name: Voyages to the Past Europe 2.dot)

© *Teacher Created Resources, Inc.* 41 *#2771 Teachers' Template Collection for Microsoft Office*

Teacher Templates for Microsoft Word

Voyages to the Past *(cont.)*

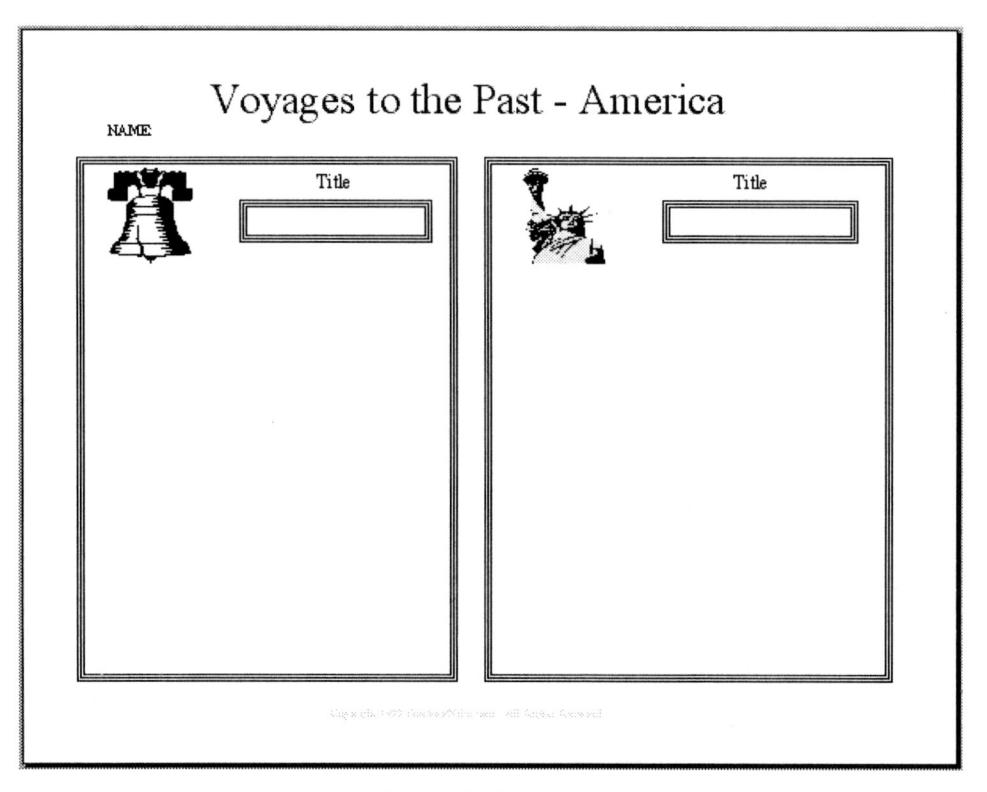

Voyages to the Past—North America (Template File Name: Voyages to the Past North America 1.dot)

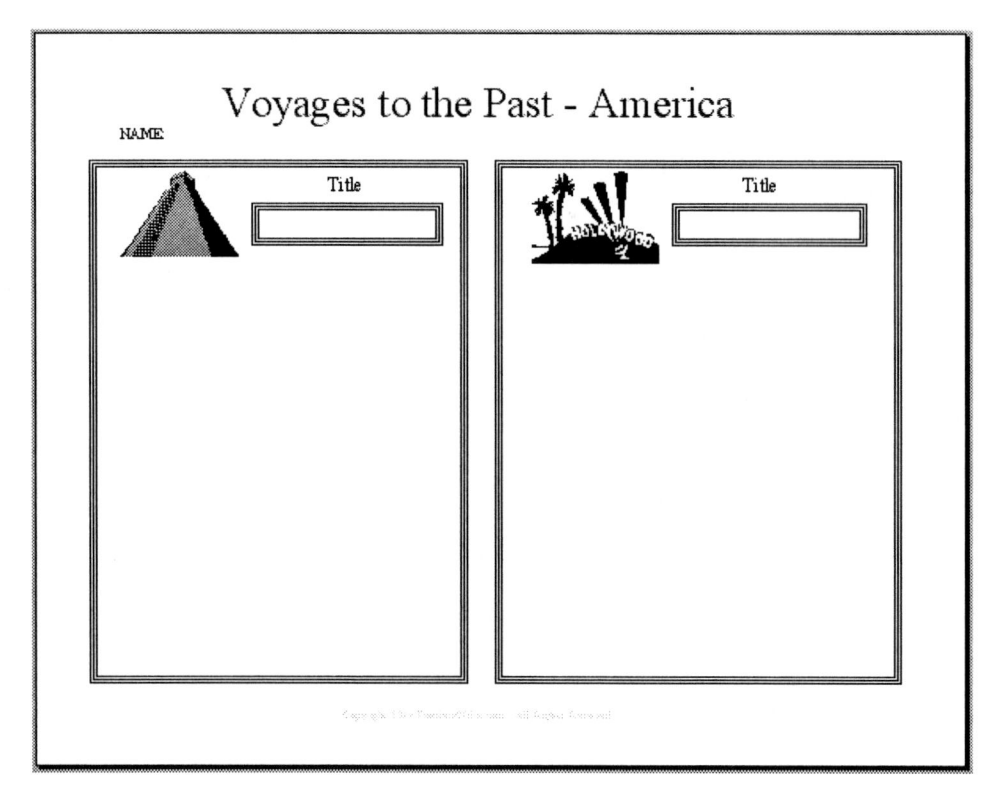

Voyages to the Past—North America (Template File Name: Voyages to the Past North America 2.dot)

Student Templates

Students benefit tremendously from working with *Microsoft Office*. From the perspective of learning a valuable work place skill, as well as using the templates designed just for students, the Student Templates Binder is a "personal learning planner" for each student.

The Student template collection contains a variety of *Word* documents that will help the student generate reports and maintain a daily journal with the use of the computer.

Student templates in *Microsoft Word* include:

- **Homework Assignments**
- **Daily Schedule**
- **Daily Journal**
- **Student Reports**
- **Study Buddies**
- **Science**

To edit these templates, students should follow the basic *Microsoft Word* operations.

1. To change or add information, click the box and enter the new information.
2. Increase or decrease text size and color by using the text options in the ***Text*** menu (Windows) or **FONT** menu (Macintosh).
3. To add or delete, click an area to highlight it, then either use the ***Copy*** and ***Paste*** features on the **EDIT** menu to add or press the **Delete** button to delete the highlighted areas.
4. To change a picture, the picture to be inserted should already have been scanned or loaded as a file on a disk or the hard drive. When they double-click the picture, students will enter the *Microsoft Clip Gallery*. Find the new picture on the computer to insert by clicking the **Import** button. After students have located the image, click **Insert**. They may have to resize or move the image once it is pasted onto the document. See the manual about importing and resizing pictures for *Microsoft Office*.

Student Templates for Microsoft Word

Student Templates *(cont.)*

Daily Journal (Template File Name: Daily Journal.dot)

Personal Journal (Template File Name: Personal Journal.dot)

Student Templates (cont.)

VOCABULARY WORDLIST

Name:

Word List 1	Word List 2	Word List 3

Copyright 1999 TeachersOffice.com All Rights Reserved

Vocabulary Word List (Template File Name: Vocabulary Wordlist.dot)

Student Templates for Microsoft Word

Student Templates (cont.)

My Schedule

Date 12/04/98 12:24 PM

Name: Bill Jones

- Science
  - Homework
- Math
  - Homework
- Social Science / History
  - Homework
- Reading / Language Arts
  - Homework
- Health
  - Homework
- Physical Education
  - Homework

Daily Schedule (Template File Name: Daily Schedule.dot)

Student Templates for Microsoft Word

Student Templates *(cont.)*

My Story

Author: David Hill   Topic: The Future

Date: 12/8/99

Are We Ready to Live in Outer Space?

My Story (Template File Name: My Story.dot)

© Teacher Created Resources, Inc.   47   #2771 Teachers' Template Collection for Microsoft Office

Student Templates for Microsoft Word

Student Templates *(cont.)*

NAME: Thomas Anders

TOPIC: Marine Life

DATE: December 12, 1998

TEACHER: Mrs. Williams

My Report

There are different types of animal life under the sea. Most of the living organisms that we're are familiar with are the many different types of fish. If you take a closer look you will discover a wide variety of life. Life under the sea is a new and exciting world. Some of these other life forms are:

Sponges
Turtles
Octopus
Kelp
Coral
Sea Lions
Whales
Star Fish
Anemones
Plankton

Student Report 1 (Template File Name: Student Report 1.dot)

Student Templates *(cont.)*

NAME: Francis Harris

TOPIC: The Space Station

DATE: December 2, 1998

TEACHER: Elizabeth Hawkins

The International Space Station

The international space station is a group project that included the Untied States and 13 other nations. Each country has committed funds and scientists to work on the complex problems of living in space. The name of this station is called Space Station Freedom. NASA believes they will have a completed station, the size of three football fields, before the year 2005. Scientists say that the station will be visible to the naked eye on earth.

Student Report 2 (Template File Name: Student Report 2.dot)

Student Templates for Microsoft Word

Student Templates (cont.)

Study Partners & Friends

Name & Address	Phone # and Email
David Smith 1236 Red Land, New York, NY 90215	202-546-8954 david@ed.com
Mary Sanders 897 Rock Rd. Lake View, NY 63254	202-548-4521

Study Buddies (Template File Name: Study Buddies.dot)

Student Templates for Microsoft Word

Science Templates

The Science template collection is a *Microsoft Word* document with clip art inserted to help students understand certain concepts in the science curriculum. The topics covered include natural science, chemistry and biology.

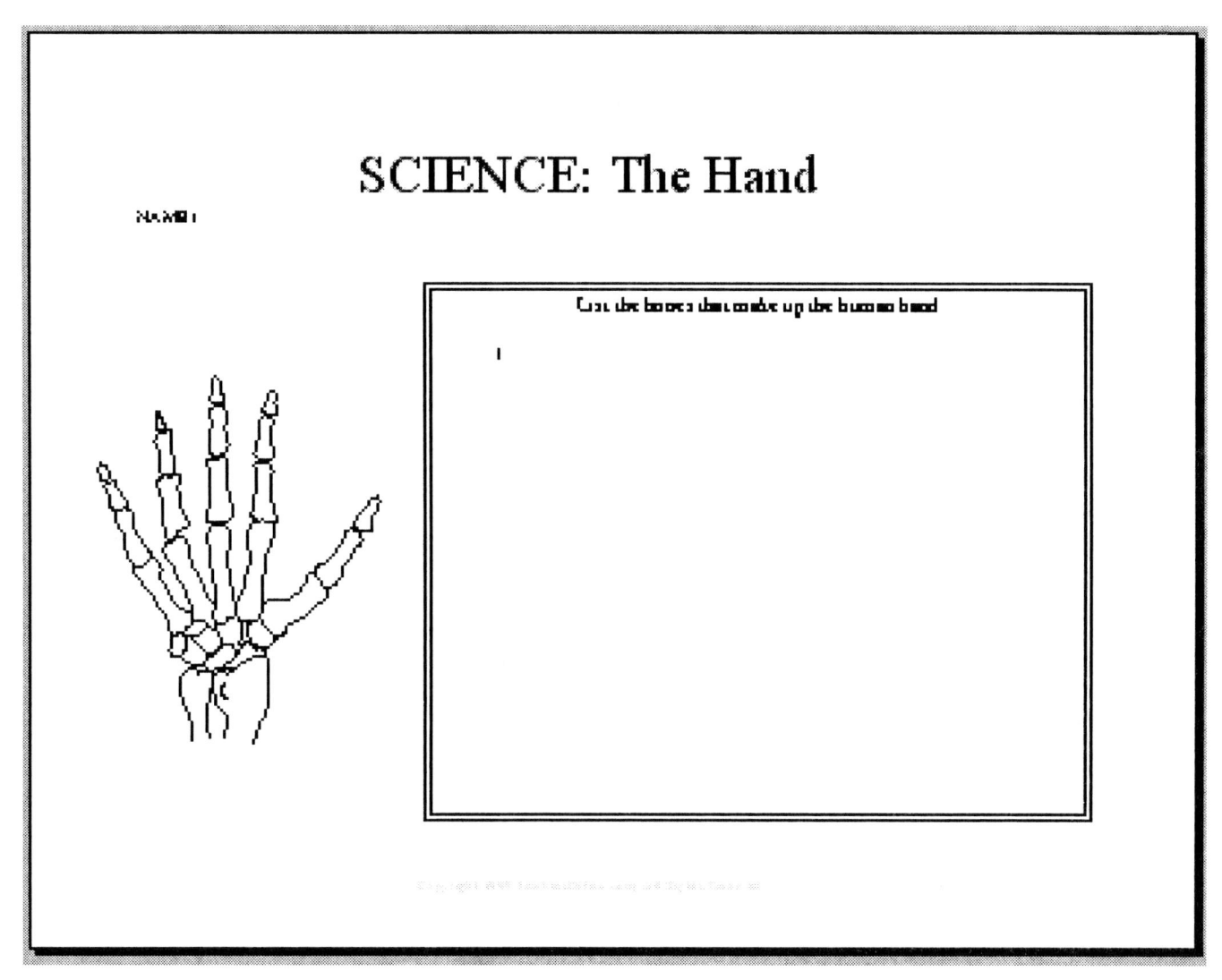

Science: The Human Hand (Template File Name: Science Anatomy Hand.dot)

© *Teacher Created Resources, Inc.* #2771 *Teachers' Template Collection for Microsoft Office*

Teacher Templates for Microsoft Word

Science Templates *(cont.)*

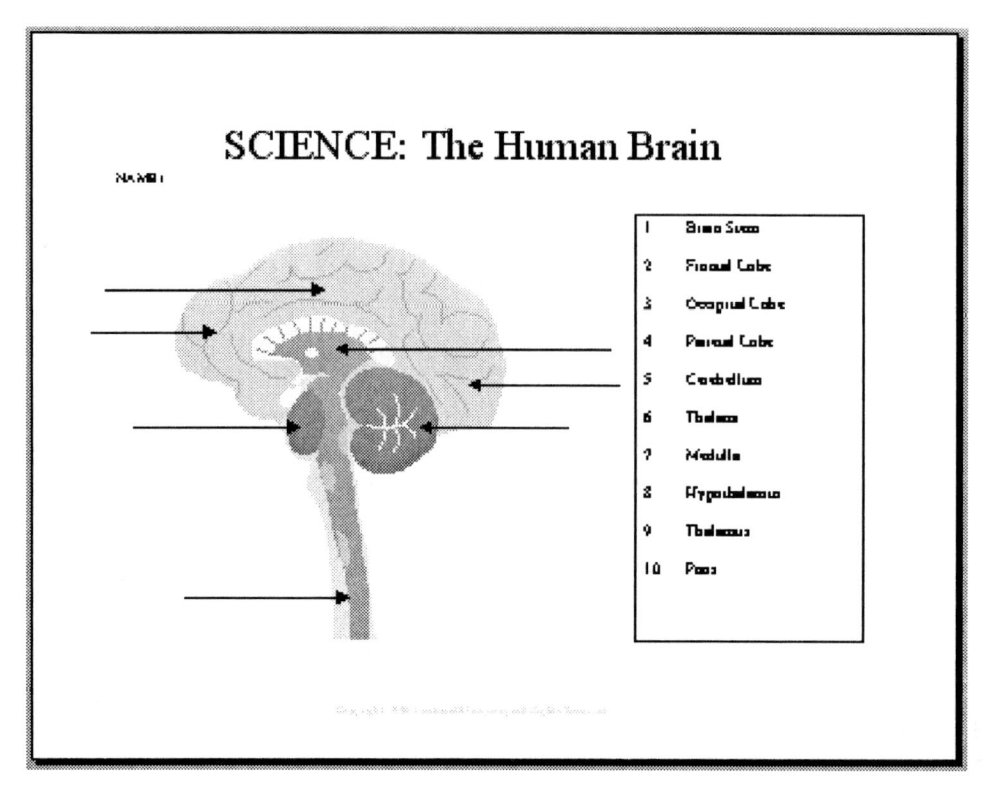

Science: The Human Brain 1 (Template File Name: Science Anatomy Brain.dot)

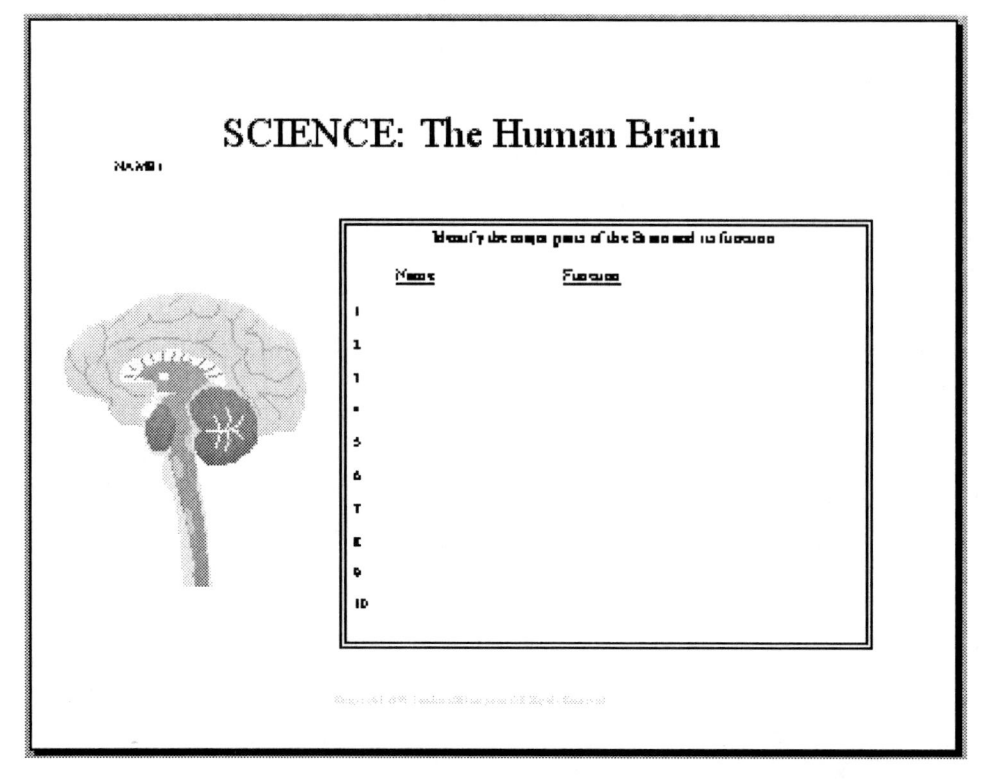

Science: The Human Brain 2 (Template File Name: Science Anatomy Brain 2.dot)

#2771 Teachers' Template Collection for Microsoft Office 52 © Teacher Created Resources, Inc.

Teacher Templates for Microsoft Word

Science Templates *(cont.)*

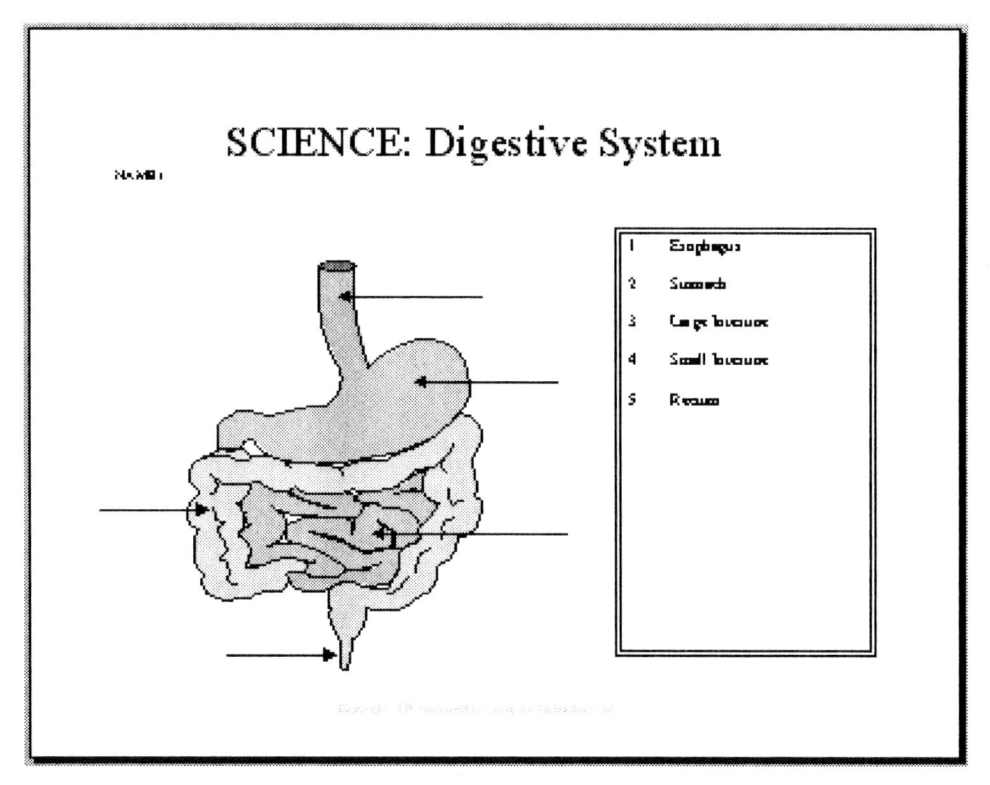

Science: Digestive System 1 (Template File Name: Science Anatomy Digestive.dot)

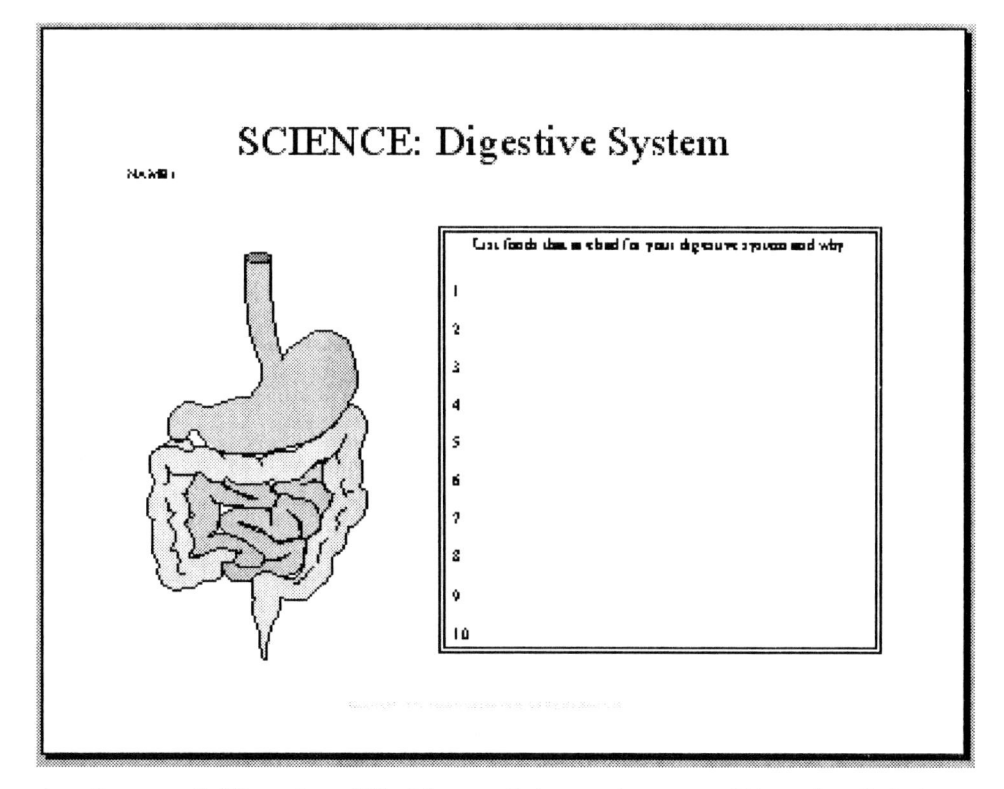

Science: Digestive System 2 (Template File Name: Science Anatomy Digestive 2.dot)

© *Teacher Created Resources, Inc.* 53 *#2771 Teachers' Template Collection for Microsoft Office*

Teacher Templates for Microsoft Word

Science Templates (cont.)

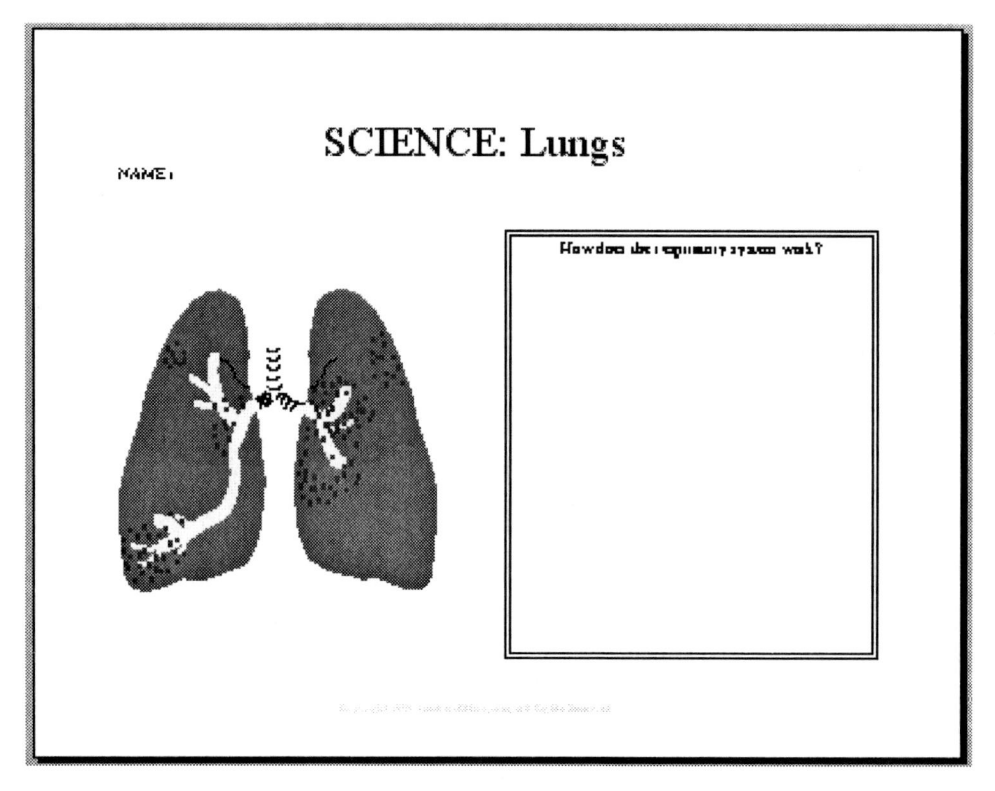

Science: The Human Lungs 1 (Template File Name: Science Anatomy Lungs.dot)

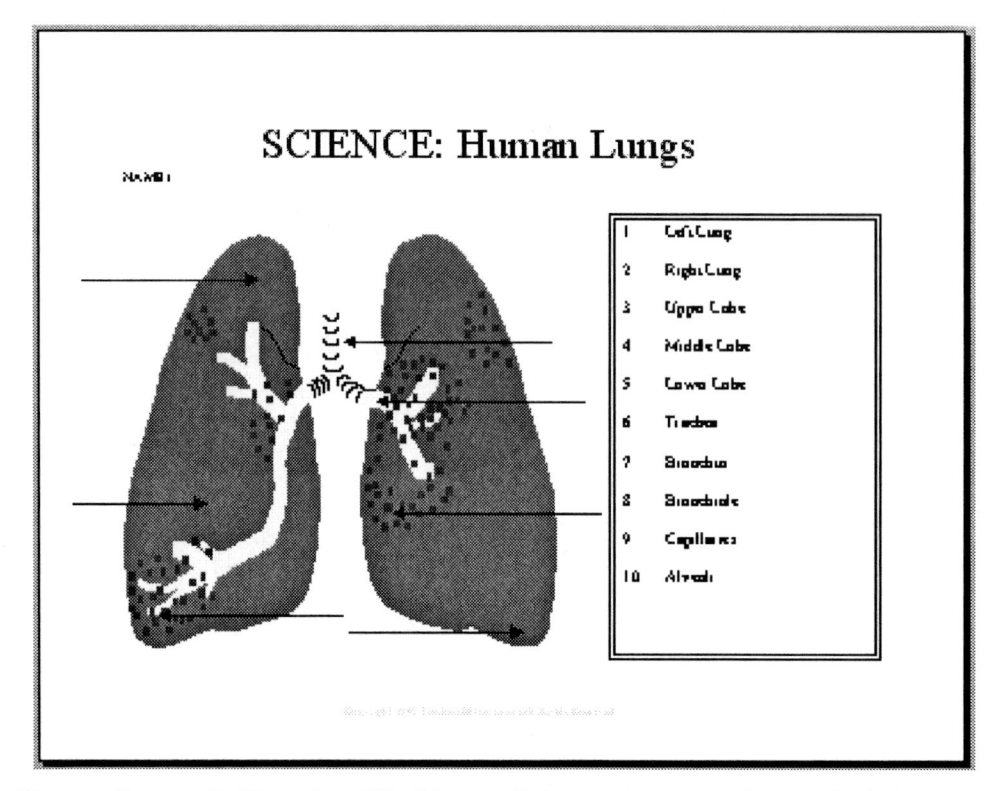

Science: The Human Lungs 2 (Template File Name: Science Anatomy Lungs 2.dot)

Teacher Templates for Microsoft Word

Science Templates *(cont.)*

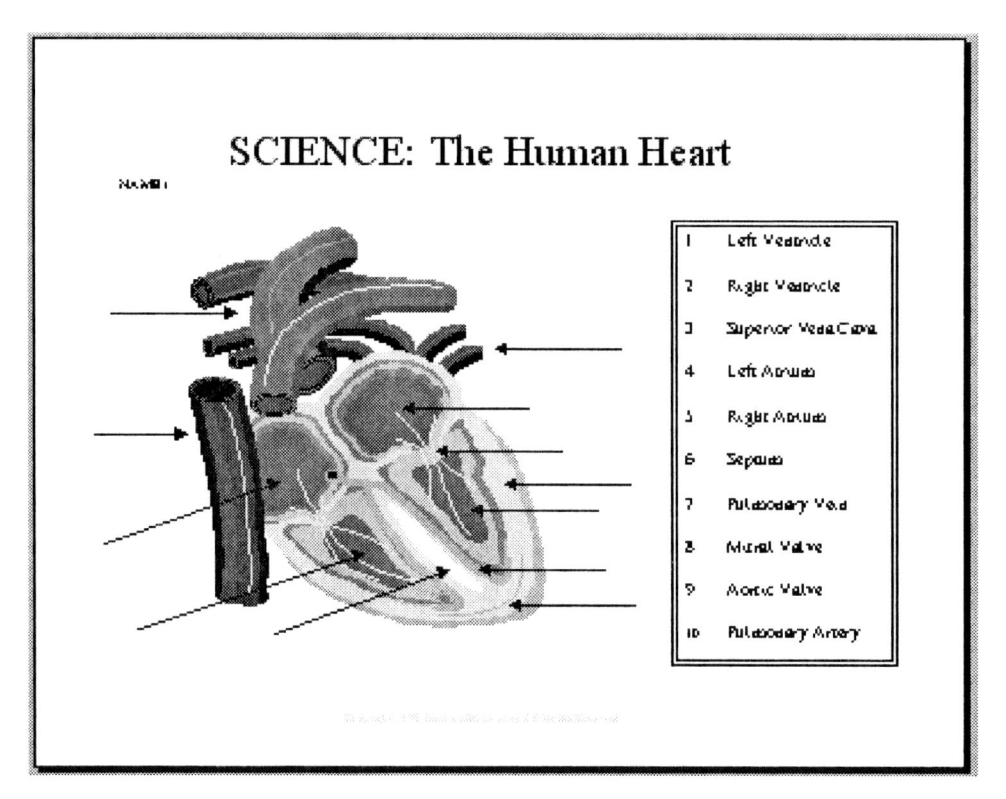

Science: The Human Heart 1 (Template File Name: Science Anatomy Heart.dot)

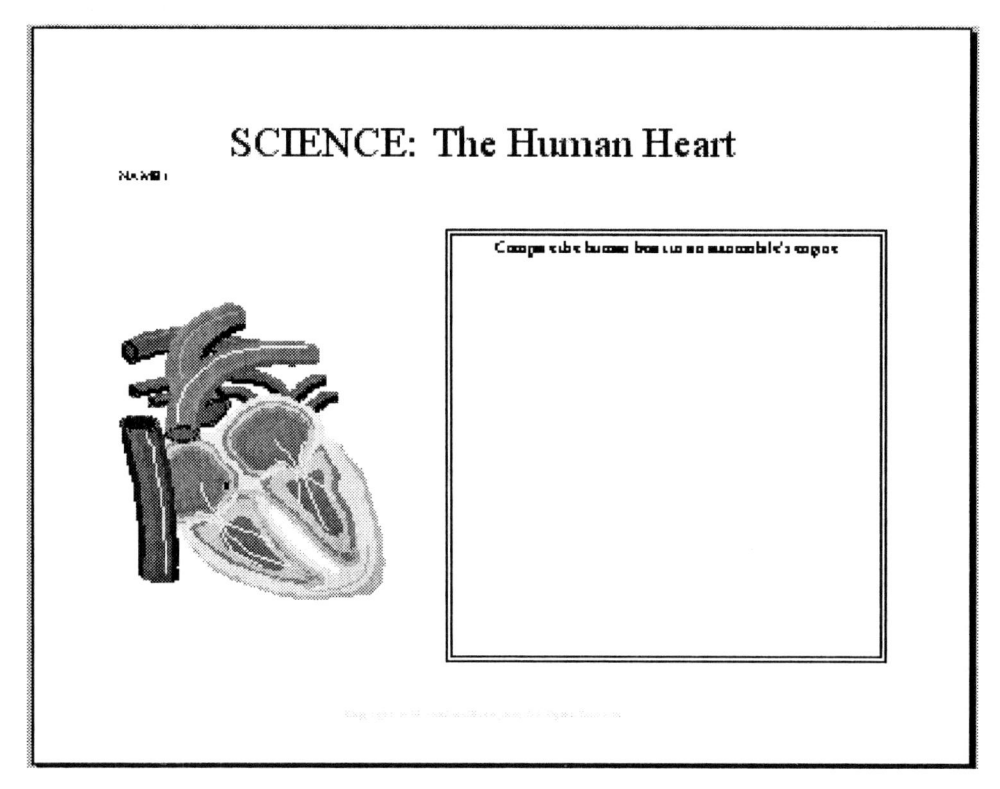

Science: The Human Heart 2 (Template File Name: Science Anatomy Heart 2.dot)

© *Teacher Created Resources, Inc.* 55 *#2771 Teachers' Template Collection for Microsoft Office*

Teacher Templates for Microsoft Word

Science Templates *(cont.)*

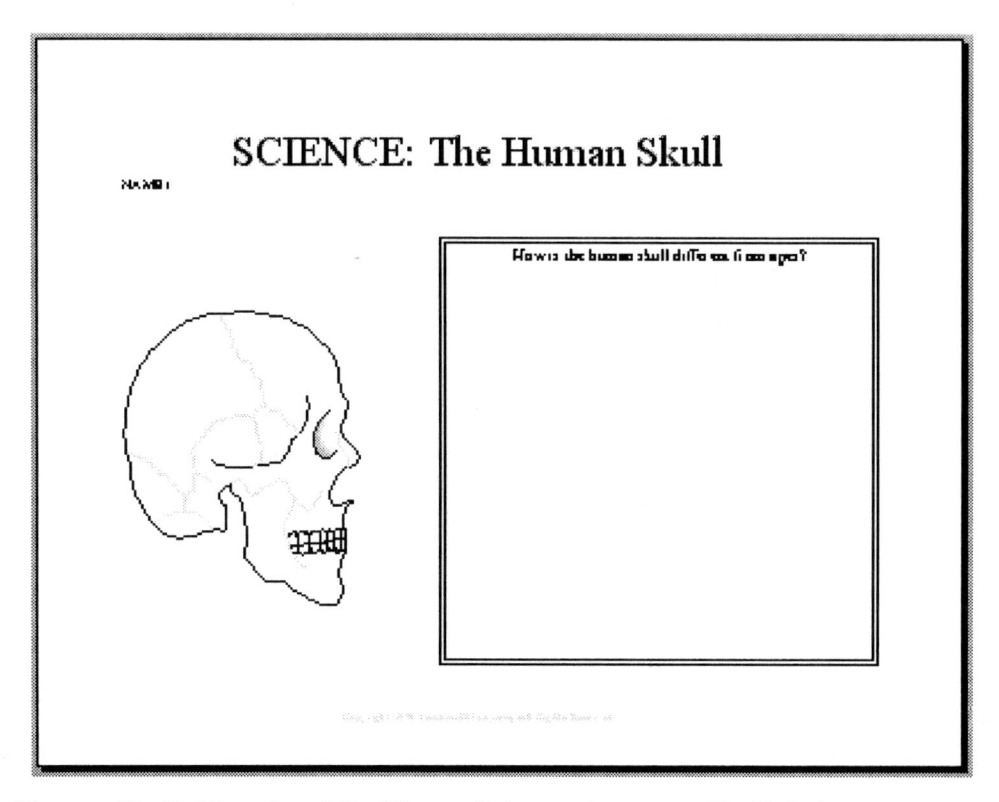

Science: The Human Skull (Template File Name: Science Anatomy Skull.dot)

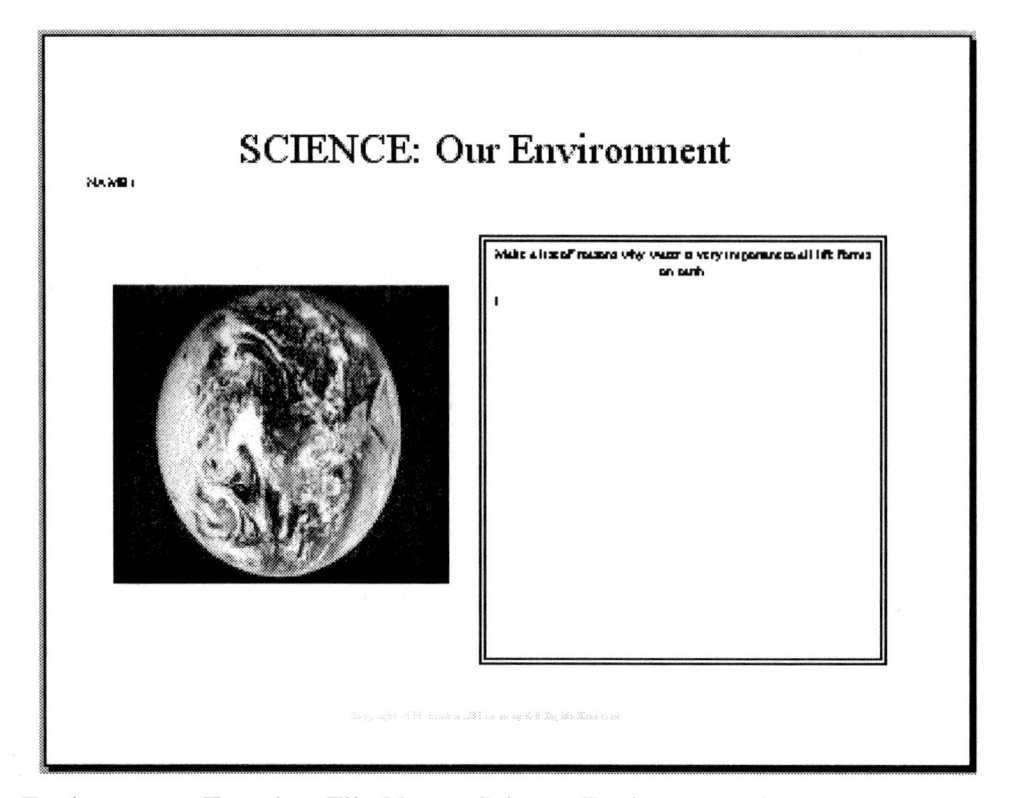

Science: The Environment (Template File Name: Science Environment.dot)

Teacher Templates for Microsoft Word

Science Templates *(cont.)*

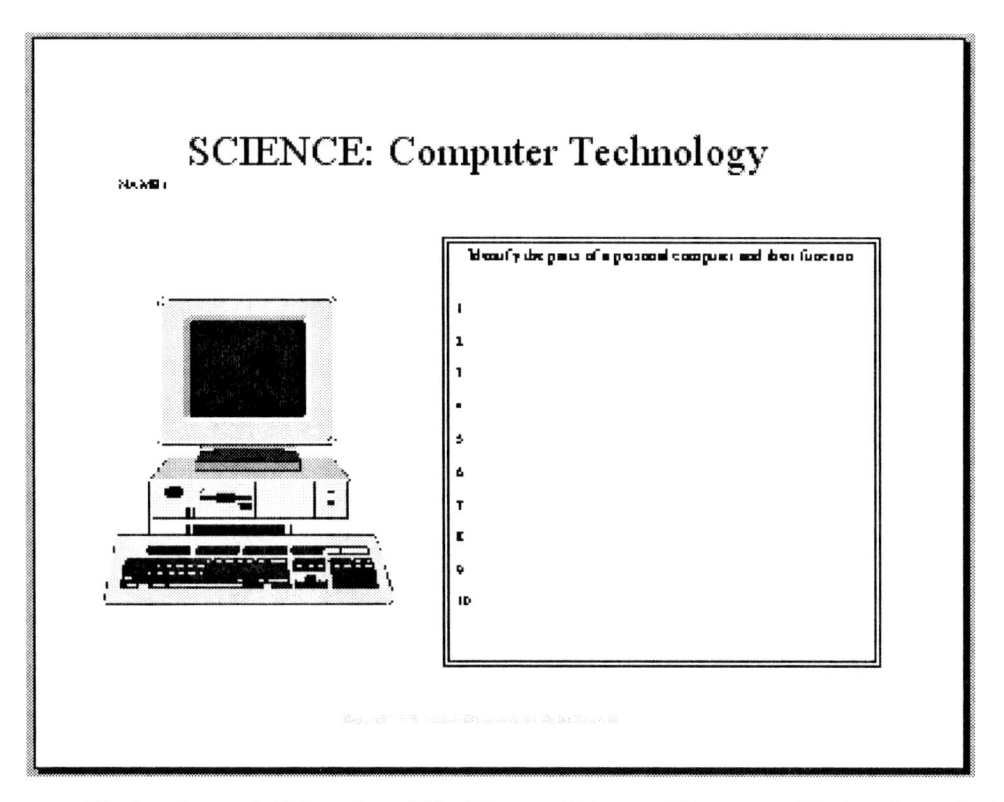

Science: Computer Technology 1 (Template File Name: Science Computer Technology.dot)

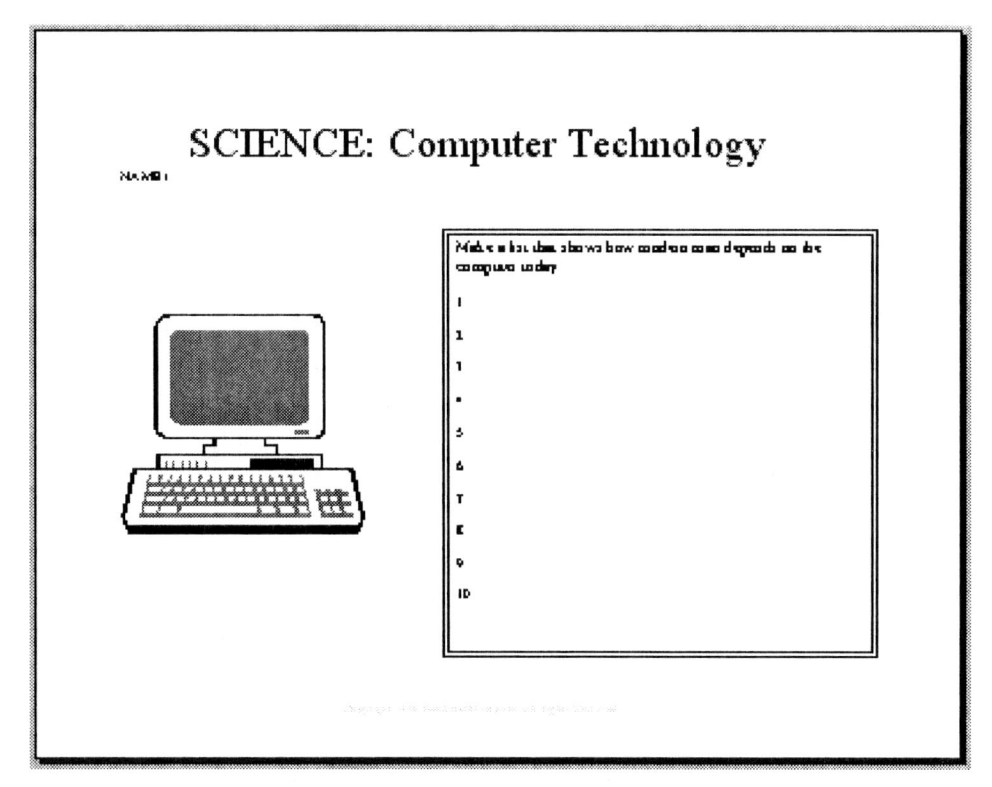

Science: Computer Technology 2 (Template File Name: Science Computer Technology 2.dot)

Teacher Templates for Microsoft Word

Science Templates *(cont.)*

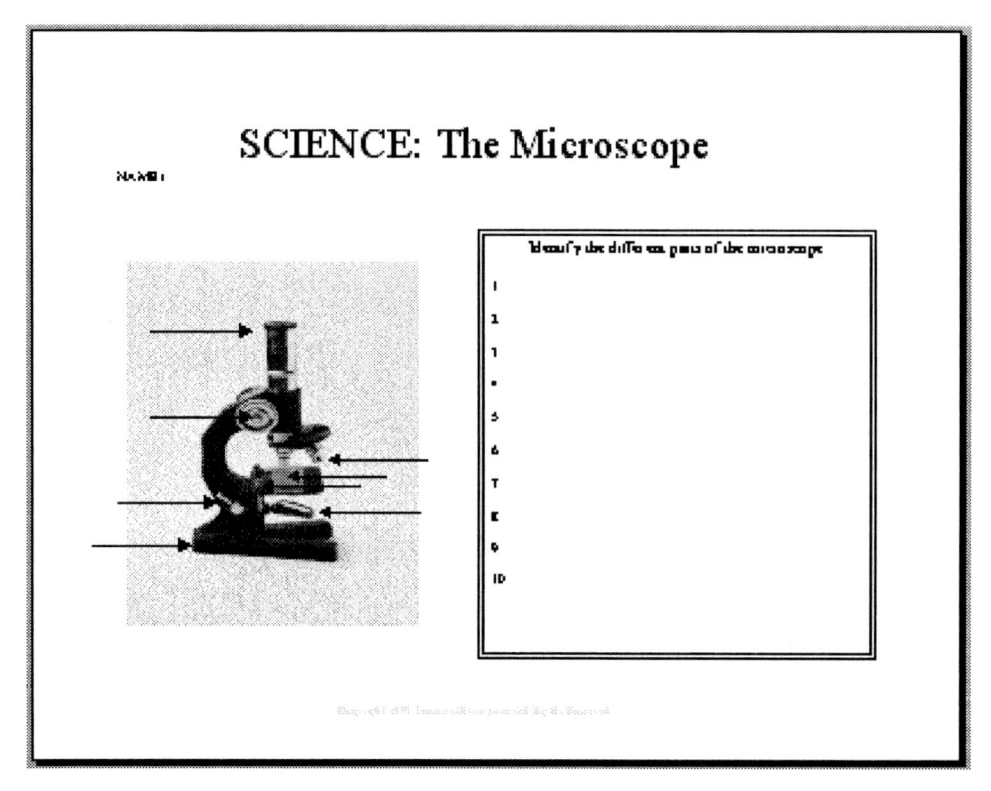

Science: The Microscope 1 (Template File Name: Science Microscope.dot)

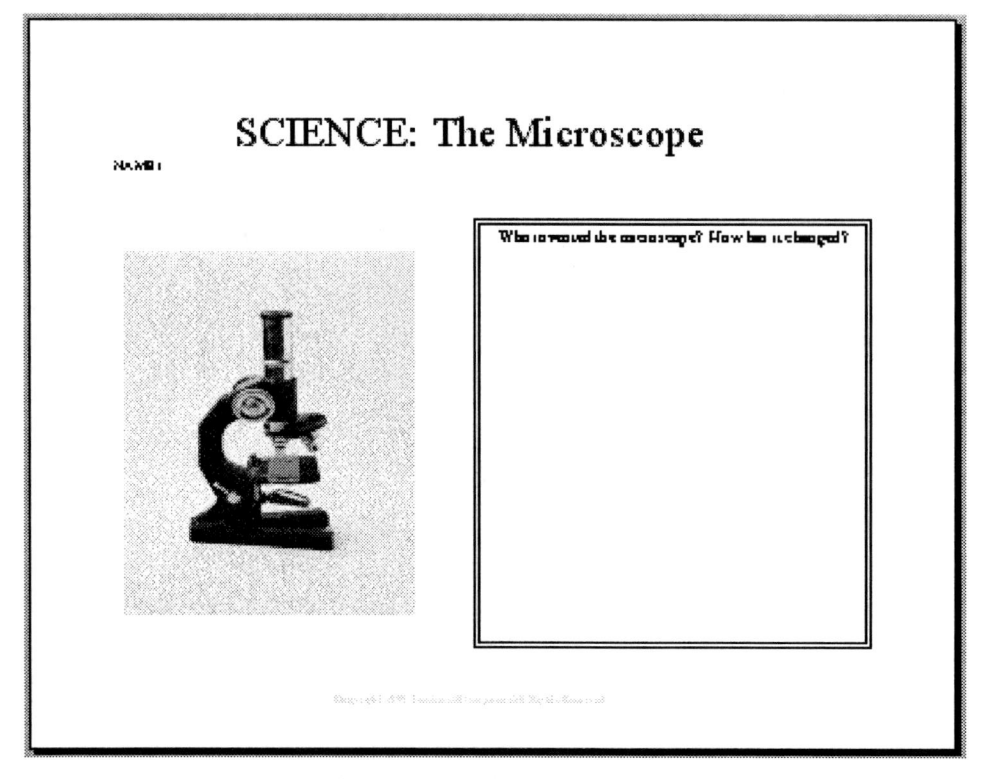

Science: The Microscope 2 (Template File Name: Science Microscope 2.dot)

Teacher Templates for Microsoft Word

Science Templates *(cont.)*

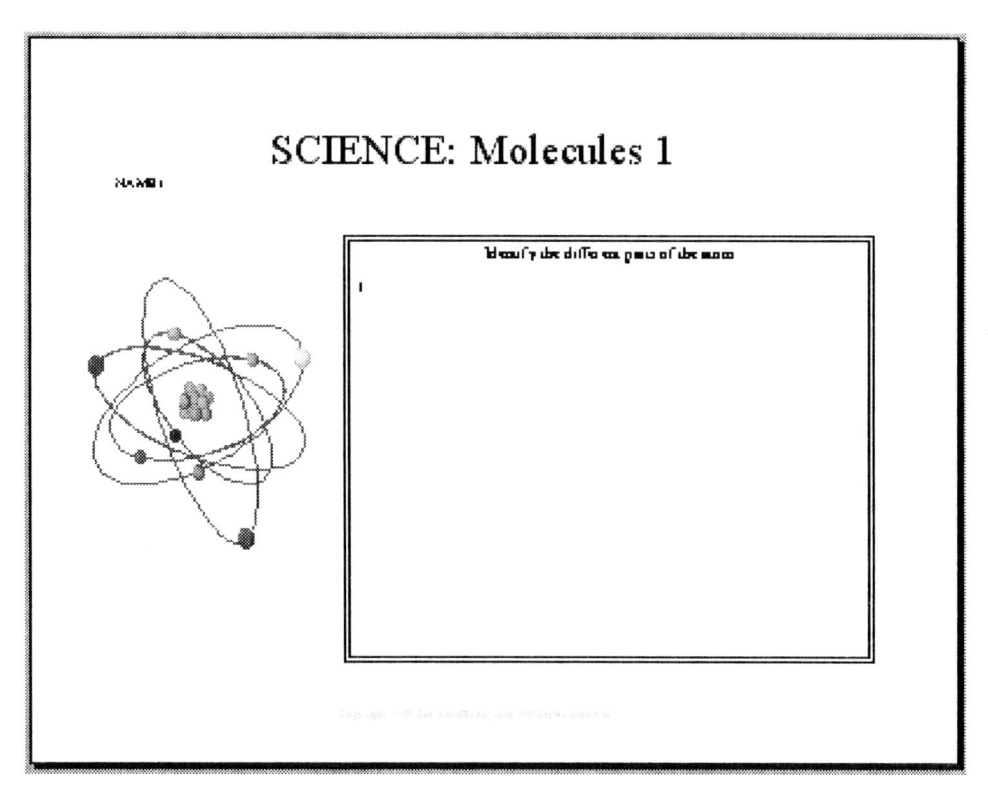

Science: Molecules 1 (Template File Name: Science Molecules 1.dot)

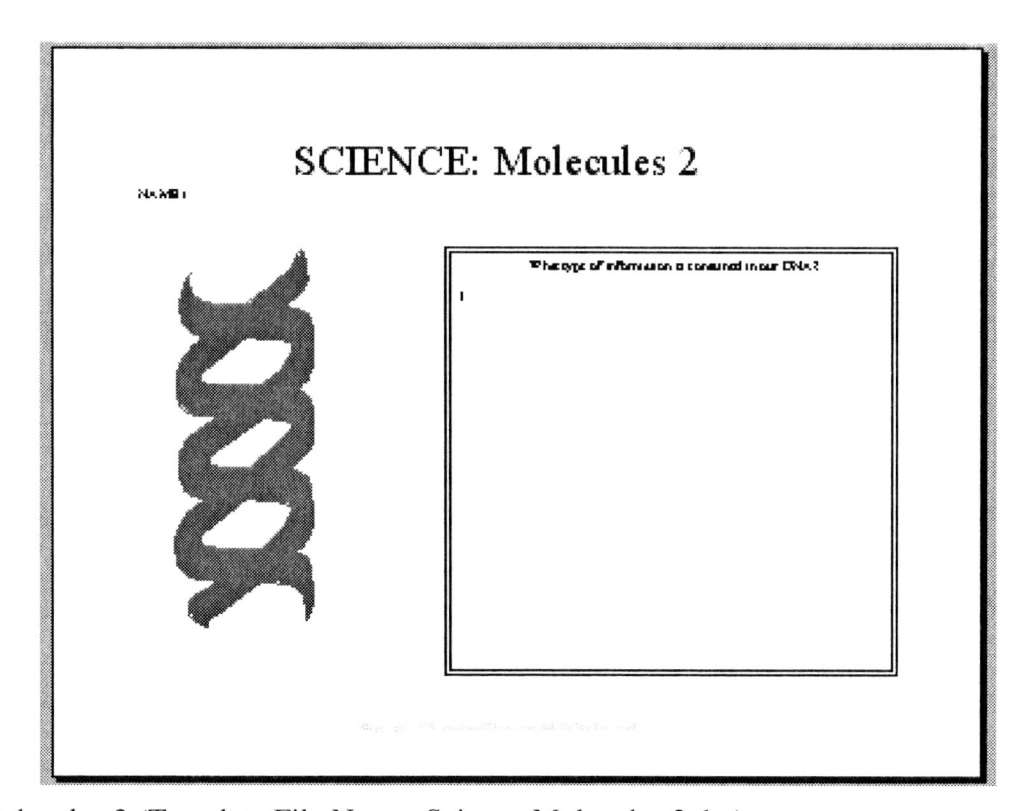

Science: Molecules 2 (Template File Name: Science Molecules 2.dot)

© *Teacher Created Resources, Inc.* 59 *#2771 Teachers' Template Collection for Microsoft Office*

Teacher Templates for Microsoft Word

Science Templates *(cont.)*

Science: Liquids (Template File Name: Science Liquids.dot)

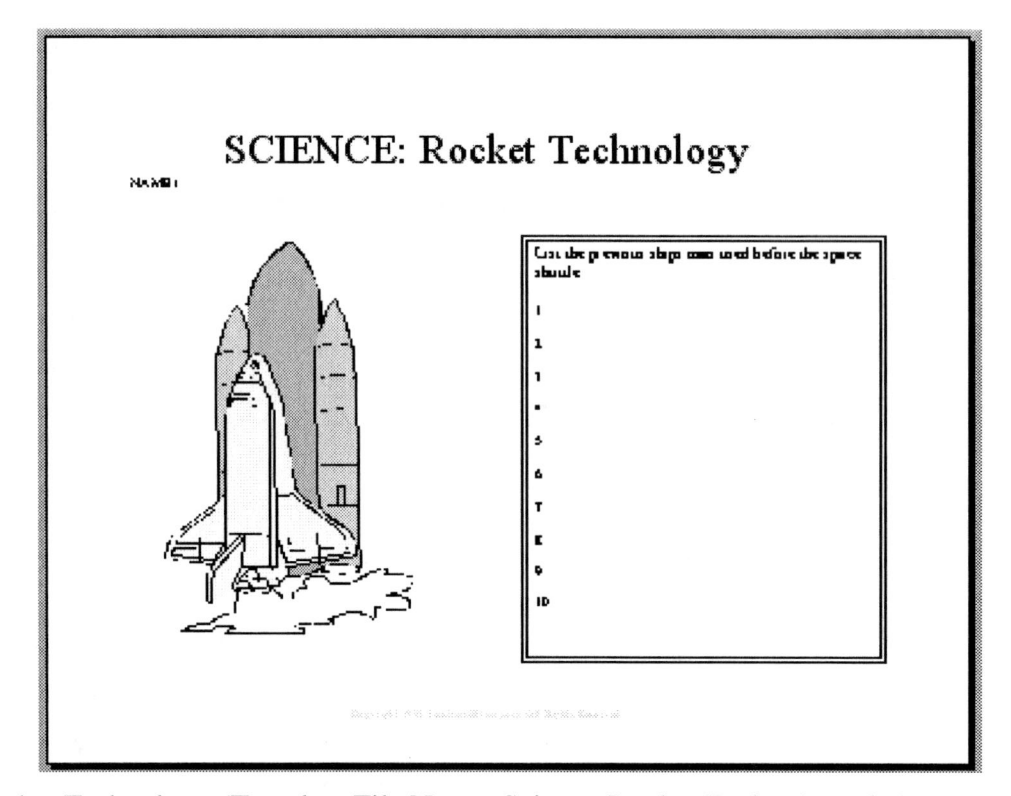

Science: Rocket Technology (Template File Name: Science Rocket Technology.dot)

Teacher Templates for Microsoft Word

Science Templates *(cont.)*

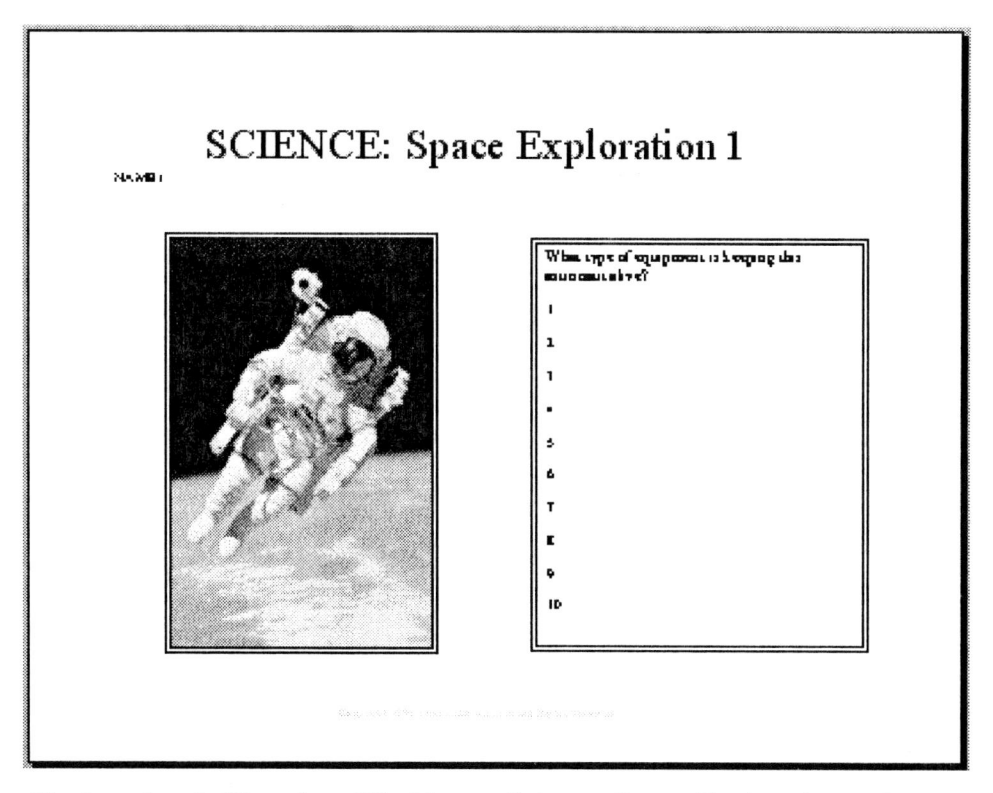

Science: Space Exploration 1 (Template File Name: Science Space Exploration 1.dot)

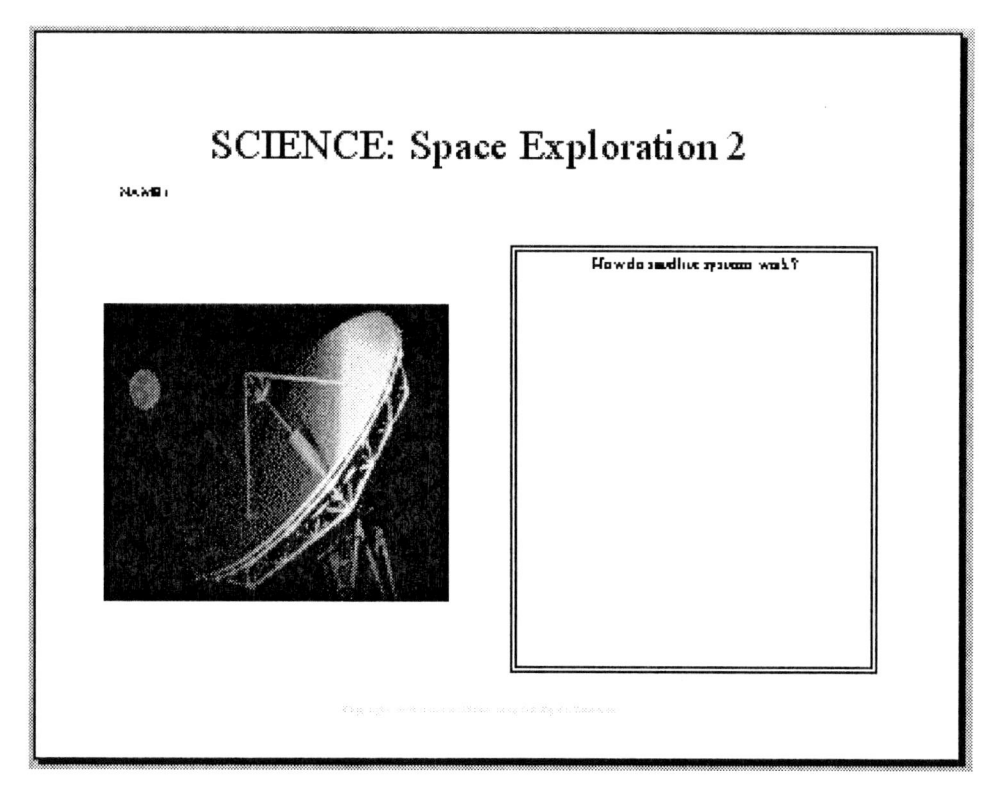

Science: Space Exploration 2 (Template File Name: Science Space Exploration 2.dot)

© *Teacher Created Resources, Inc.* 61 *#2771 Teachers' Template Collection for Microsoft Office*

Teacher Templates for Microsoft Word

Science Templates *(cont.)*

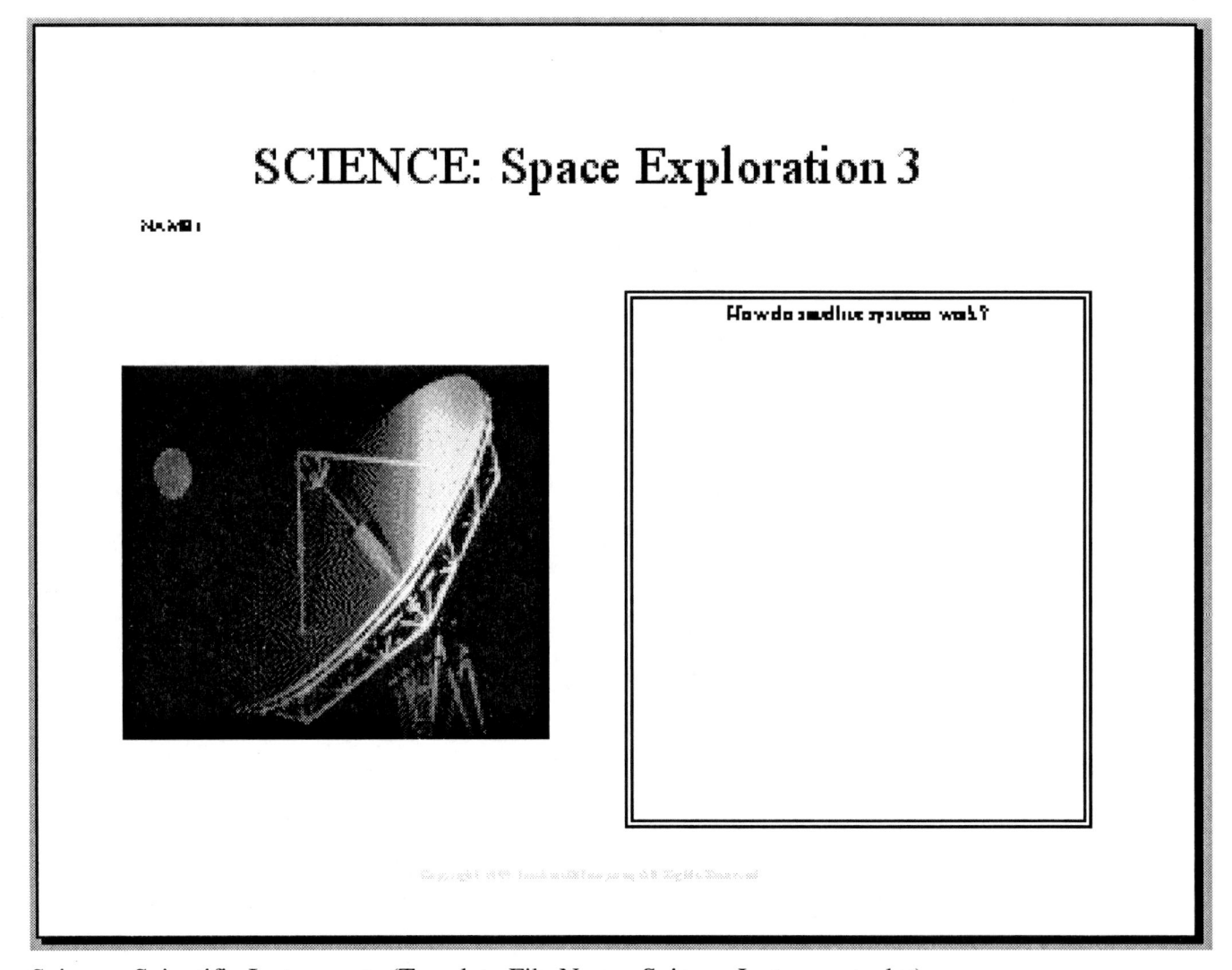

Science: Scientific Instruments (Template File Name: Science Instruments.dot)

Teacher Templates for Microsoft PowerPoint

The *Microsoft PowerPoint* templates contain presentations for teachers and students. These *Microsoft PowerPoint* presentations can be edited to modify content and style to your own specifications and are geared for immediate use. These templates are designed to help teachers understand the power of *Microsoft PowerPoint* and its multimedia applications.

Teachers can use the following presentations in the classroom:

- Marine Biology Presentation: contains video and still images of marine biology.
- Open House Presentation: contains a sample presentation of faculty and student activities that can be used for school or community events.
- Student Awards Presentation: contains a slideshow to recognize students based on different topics; an excellent way to highlight achievement at parent meetings, open house and conferences.
- Department Resource Presentation: contains a sample presentation departments can modify to highlight curriculum, faculty, course outlines, and schedules of classes. It can also be used as a school web site when converted into an HTML file.
- Social Studies Presentation: contains images of Meso-American cultures.

Students can use the following presentations in the classroom:

- Family Tree Presentation: contains images and stories of a sample family history.
- A Day at the Zoo Presentation: contains sound and images of animals found at a typical zoo.
- Storybook Maker Presentation: contains drawings with balloon text to help model story writing.
- Study Guide Presentation: contains helpful hints for students and samples of information to which students can refer to complete assignments.
- Electronic Yearbook Presentation: contains pictures and video demonstrating how a school or class can create an electronic yearbook using multimedia.

These presentations will enhance student productivity by incorporating various media (sound, video, still images, clip art) into their course curriculum. Students will be motivated to integrate these concepts into their work. Their projects can then be used outside of the classroom environment when *Microsoft PowerPoint Player* is included with the presentations. Students can create a collection of their presentations and use it as a personal student portfolio.

Both students and teachers can use all of the template presentations. With *Microsoft PowerPoint*, classroom presentations will never be the same.

Teacher Templates for Microsoft PowerPoint *(cont.)*

Note: All presentations have animation features attached to selected screens. To change an animation effect, go to the menu bar and select SLIDE SHOW from the menu options. Select Custom Animation, and then select Effects. You can change any effect programmed into the template presentation from this point. Refer to your *Microsoft PowerPoint* manual for detailed explanations on using animation features and importing audio and video samples into your presentations.

If you choose to change the video clips, remember to double-click on the existing videos and replace them with videos (AVI files) from the *Microsoft Clip Gallery* or from a file on the hard disk. To store your presentation on another disk or to load it on another computer, remember to add the AVI files along with the presentation file. The *Microsoft PowerPoint Player* that allows you to play your presentations has been included on the CD-ROM. To use the *Microsoft PowerPoint Player*, you will need to save your presentations as a PowerPoint Show file and include the player with your PowerPoint Show file when you save to a hard drive or Zip disk.

The following pages are sample screens from each of the Presentation template files.

Teacher Templates for Microsoft PowerPoint

Teacher Presentation Templates

Open House Presentation

Open House (Opening Screen. Template File Name: Open House 2.pot)

Teacher Templates for Microsoft PowerPoint

Teacher Presentation Templates (cont.)

Open House Presentation

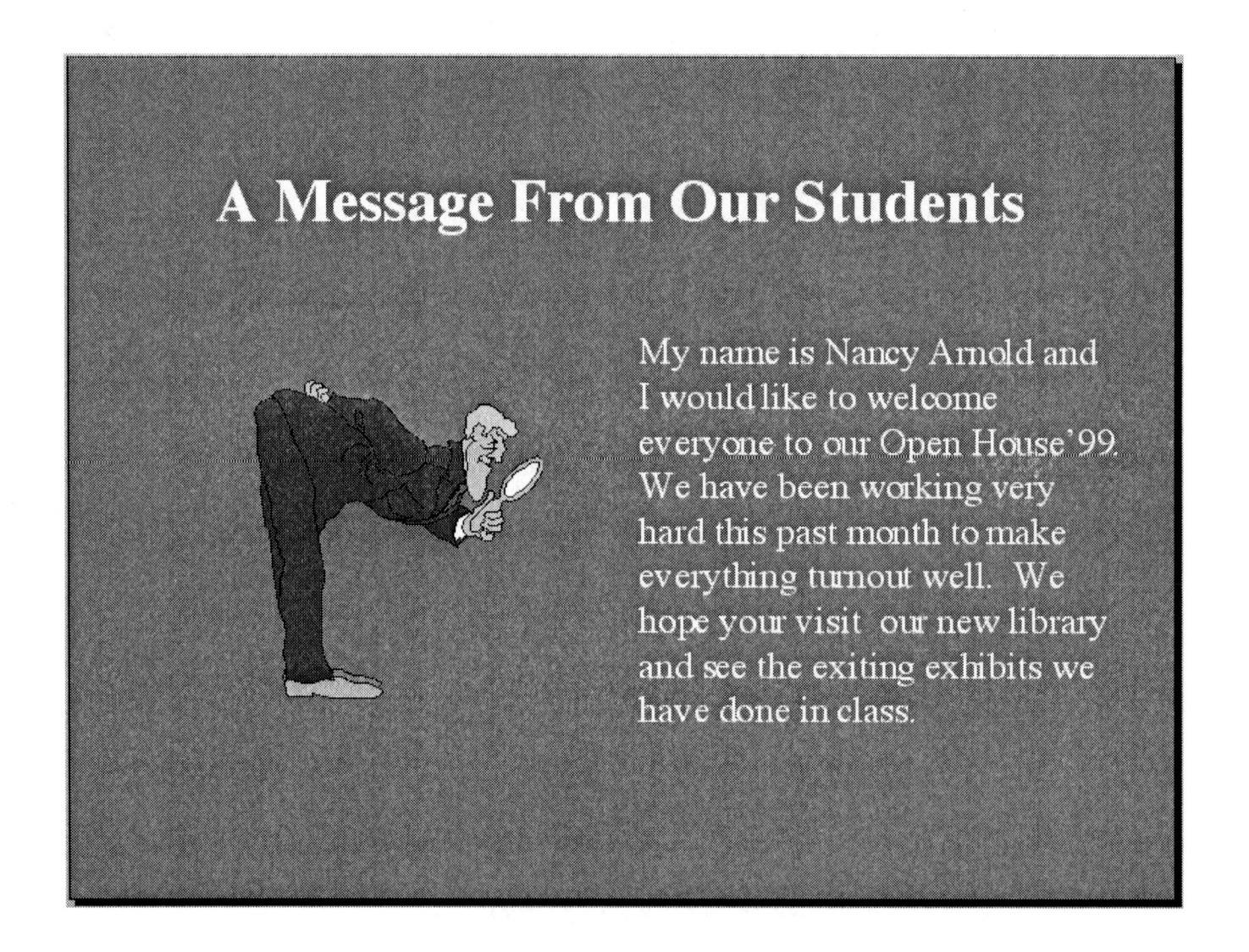

A Message From Our Students

My name is Nancy Arnold and I would like to welcome everyone to our Open House '99. We have been working very hard this past month to make everything turnout well. We hope your visit our new library and see the exiting exhibits we have done in class.

Teacher Templates for Microsoft PowerPoint

Teacher Presentation Templates *(cont.)*

Open House Presentation *(cont.)*

George Washington Administrators

Mrs. Roland
Assistant Principal

Mr. Griffen
Assistant Principal

Teacher Templates for Microsoft PowerPoint

Teacher Presentation Templates *(cont.)*

Open House Presentation *(cont.)*

George Washington Library

G.W. Library is in the process of adding more computers to meet the needs of our community. Come by and visit our new Parent Center located by the stadium.

Teacher Templates for Microsoft PowerPoint

Teacher Presentation Templates *(cont.)*

Student Awards Presentation

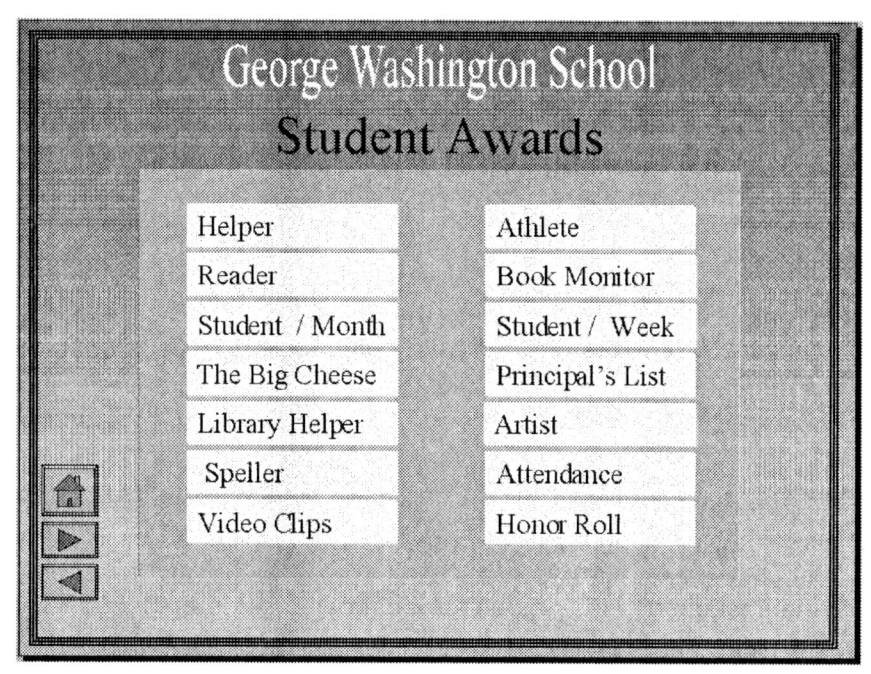

Student Awards (Opening Screen. Template File Name: Student Awards Collection.pot)

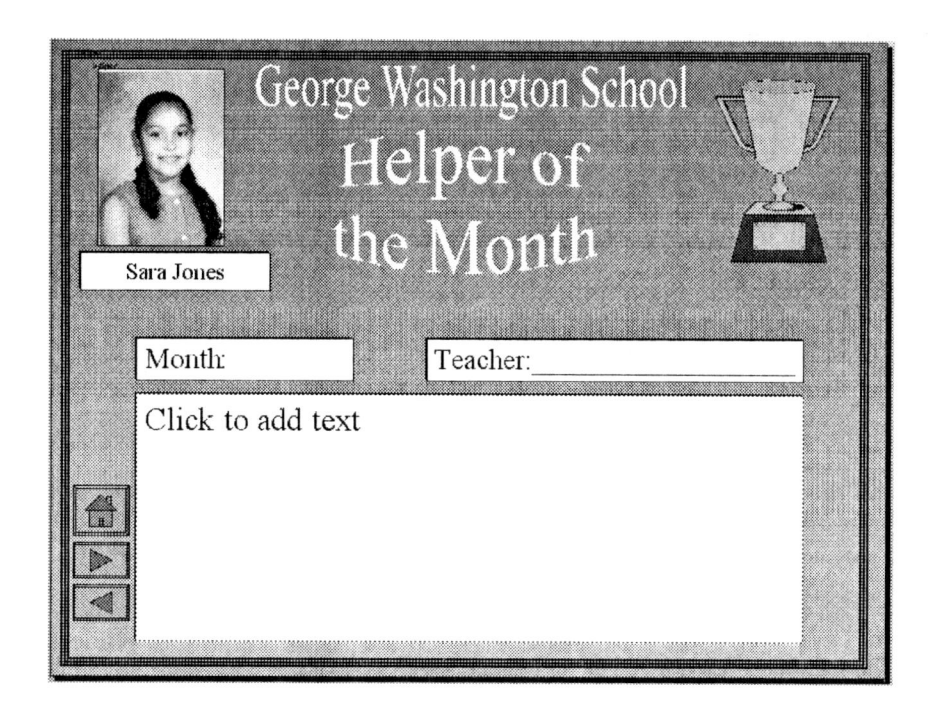

© *Teacher Created Resources, Inc.* 69 *#2771 Teachers' Template Collection for Microsoft Office*

Teacher Templates for Microsoft PowerPoint

Teacher Presentation Templates *(cont.)*

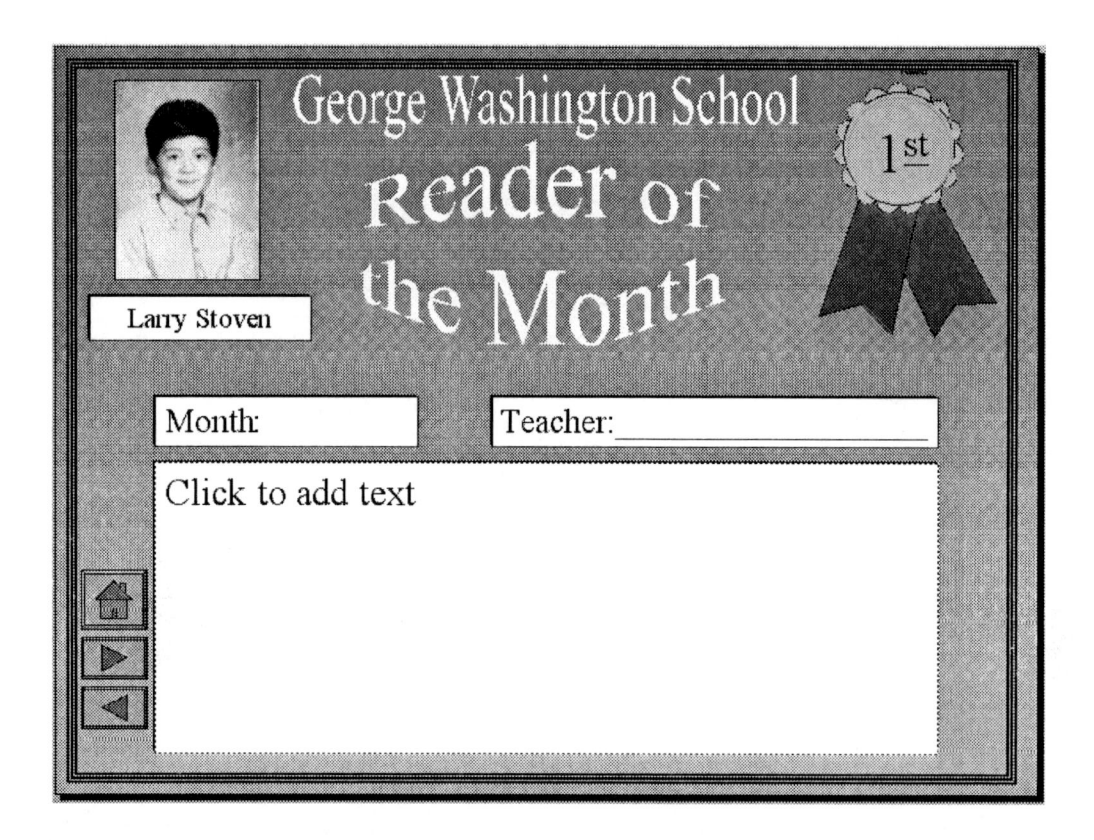

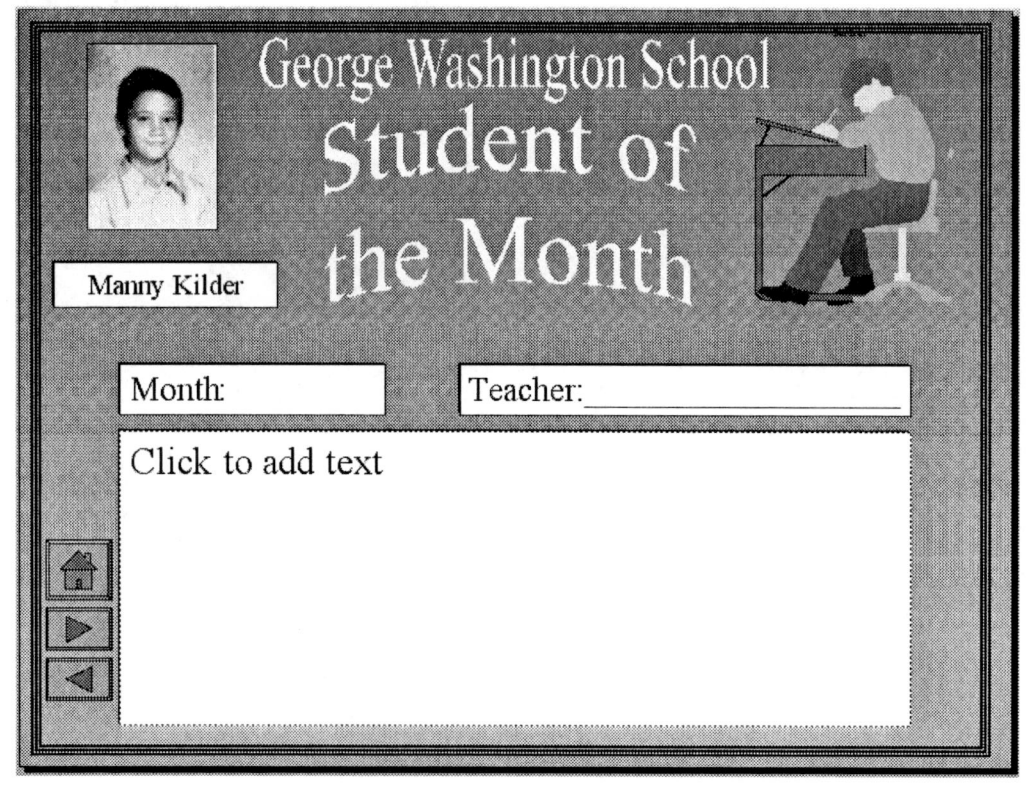

George Washington School
Reader of the Month

Larry Stoven

Month: Teacher:

Click to add text

George Washington School
Student of the Month

Manny Kilder

Month: Teacher:

Click to add text

#2771 Teachers' Template Collection for Microsoft Office © Teacher Created Resources, Inc.

Teacher Templates for Microsoft PowerPoint

Teacher Presentation Templates *(cont.)*

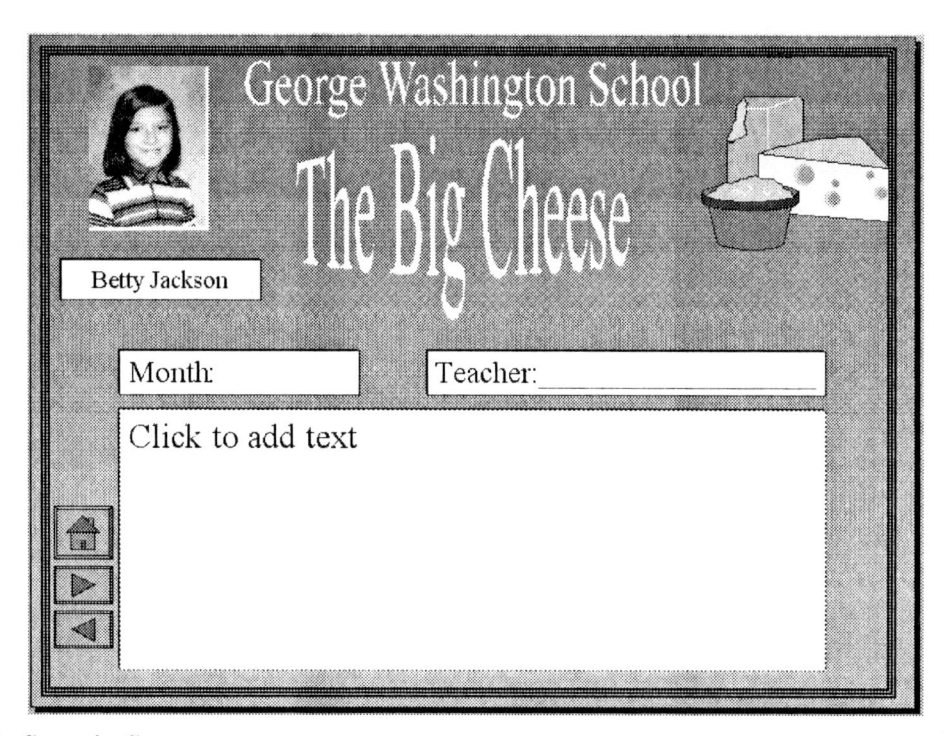

Student Awards Sample Screens

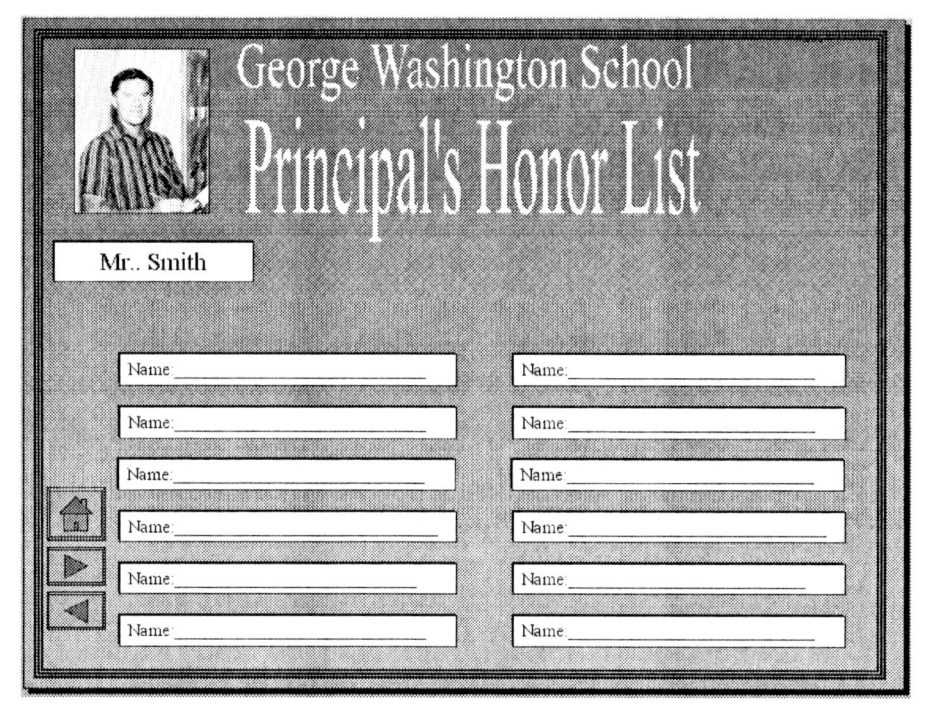

Student Awards Sample Screens

© *Teacher Created Resources, Inc.*   71   #2771 *Teachers' Template Collection for Microsoft Office*

Teacher Templates for Microsoft PowerPoint

Teacher Presentation Templates *(cont.)*

Department Resource Presentation

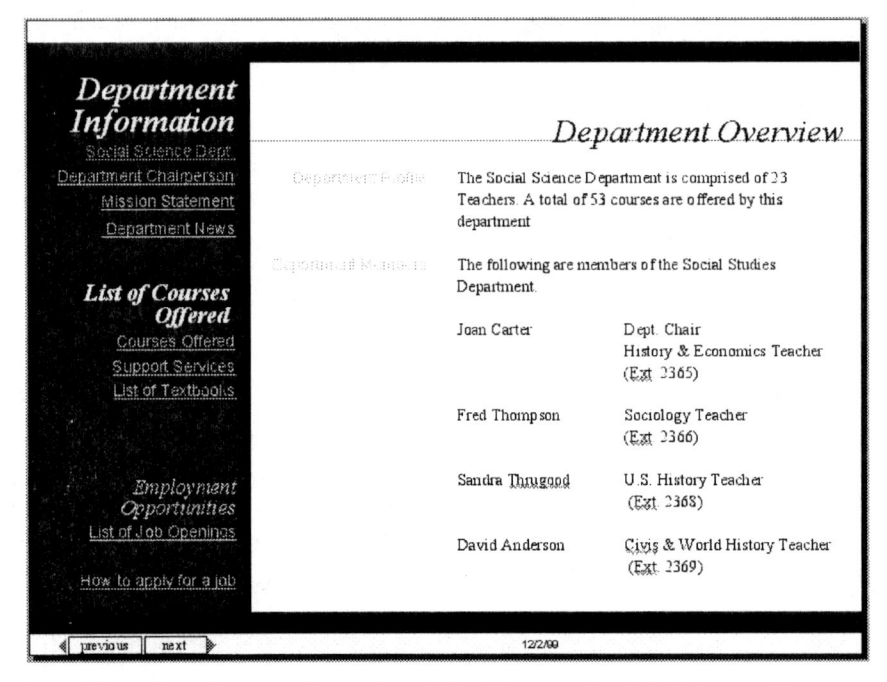

Department Overview (Opening Screen. Template File Name: Social Science Department Info.pot)

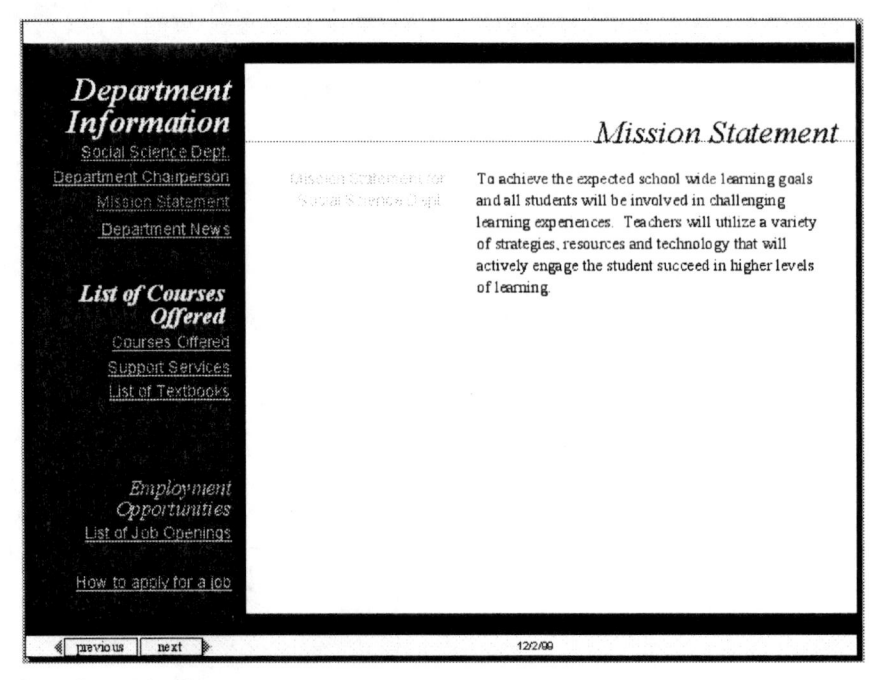

Department Overview Sample Screen

#2771 Teachers' Template Collection for Microsoft Office © Teacher Created Resources, Inc.

Teacher Templates for Microsoft PowerPoint

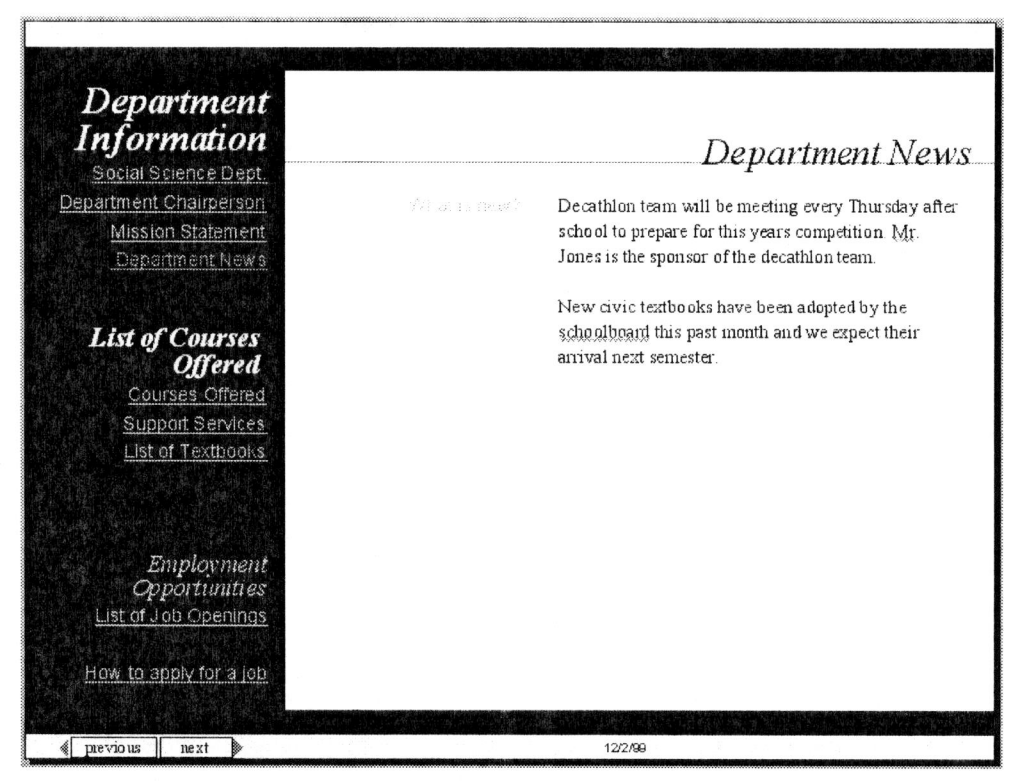

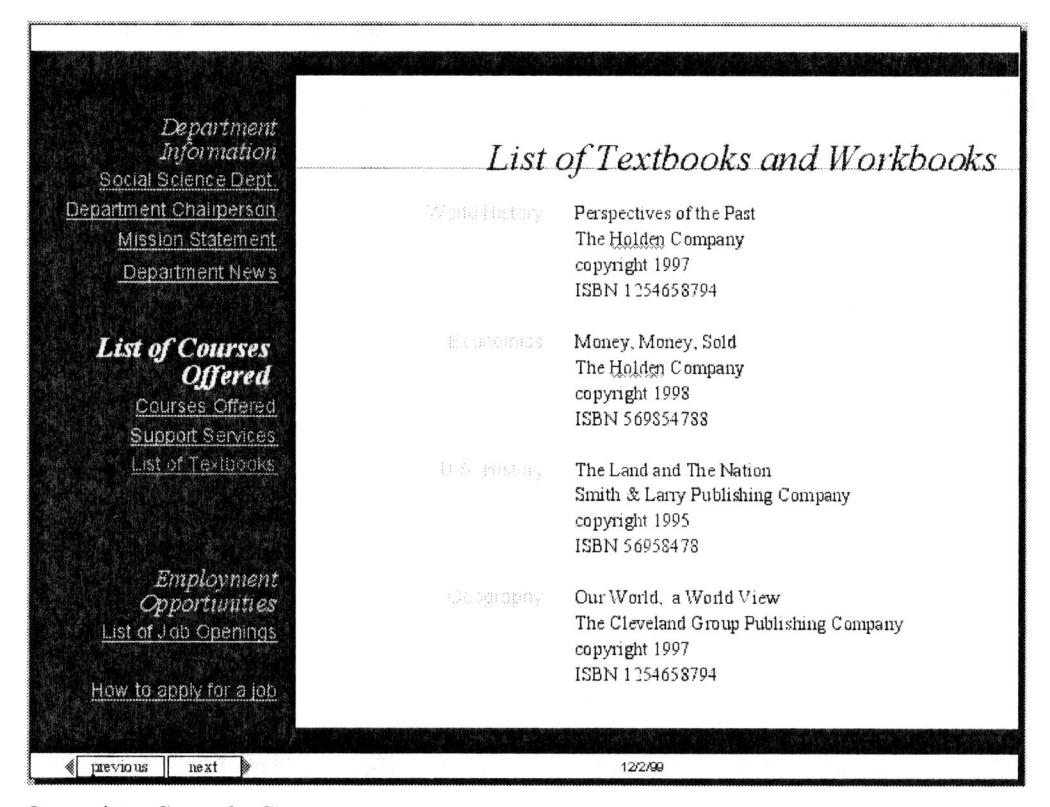

Teacher Presentation Templates (cont.)

Department Overview Sample Screen

Department Overview Sample Screen

Teacher Templates for Microsoft PowerPoint

Teacher Presentation Templates *(cont.)*

Lesson Presentation Template (Oceans)

Marine Biology (Opening Screen. Template File Name: Marine Biology.pot)

Marine Biology Sample Screen

Teacher Templates for Microsoft PowerPoint

Teacher Presentation Templates *(cont.)*

Lesson Presentation Template (Social Studies)

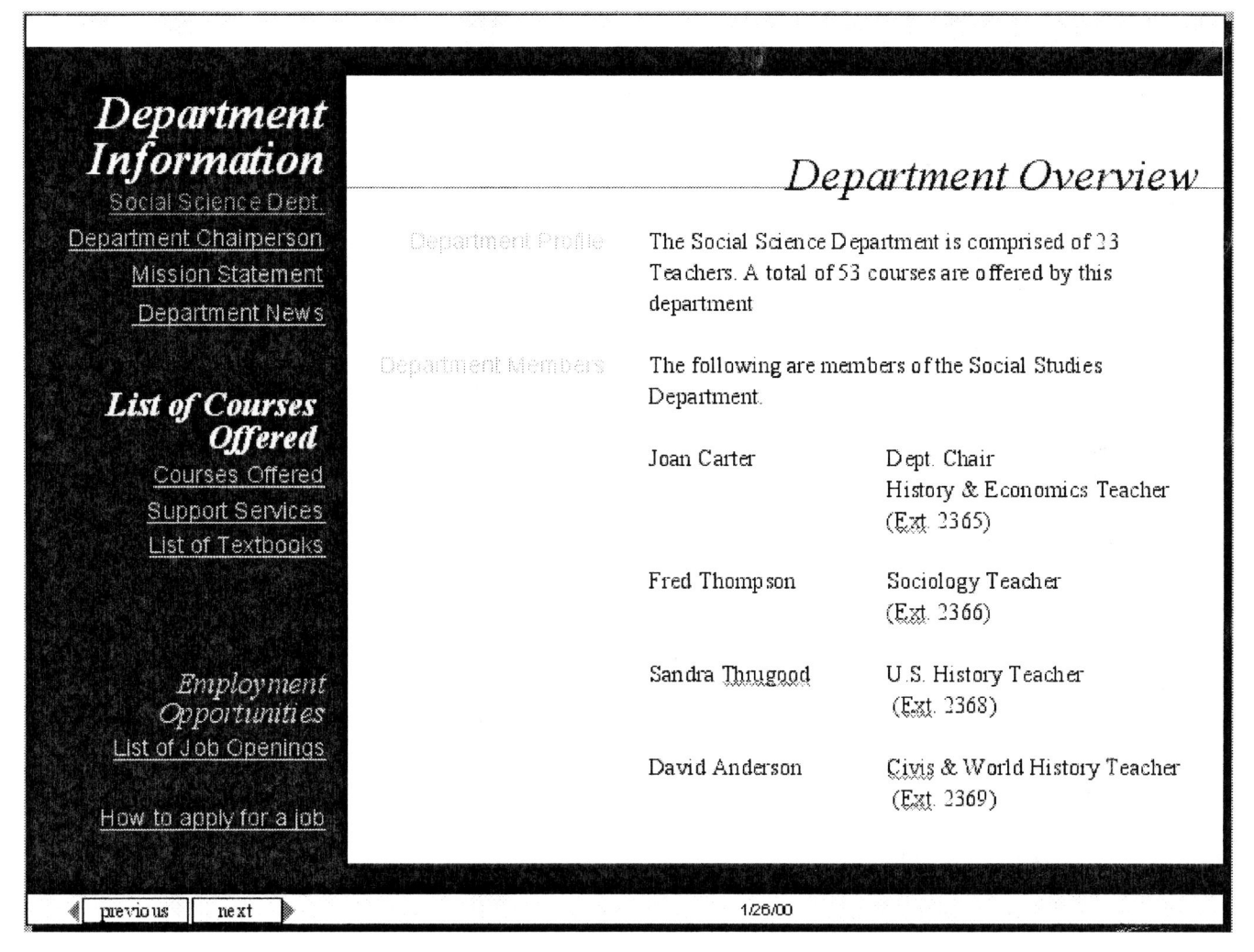

Department Information
- Social Science Dept.
- Department Chairperson
- Mission Statement
- Department News

List of Courses Offered
- Courses Offered
- Support Services
- List of Textbooks

Employment Opportunities
- List of Job Openings
- How to apply for a job

Department Overview

Department Profile: The Social Science Department is comprised of 23 Teachers. A total of 53 courses are offered by this department

Department Members: The following are members of the Social Studies Department.

Joan Carter	Dept. Chair / History & Economics Teacher (Ext. 2365)
Fred Thompson	Sociology Teacher (Ext. 2366)
Sandra Thrugood	U.S. History Teacher (Ext. 2368)
David Anderson	Civis & World History Teacher (Ext. 2369)

1/26/00

Social Studies (Opening Screen. (Template File Name: Social Science.pot)

Teacher Templates for Microsoft PowerPoint

Teacher Presentation Templates *(cont.)*

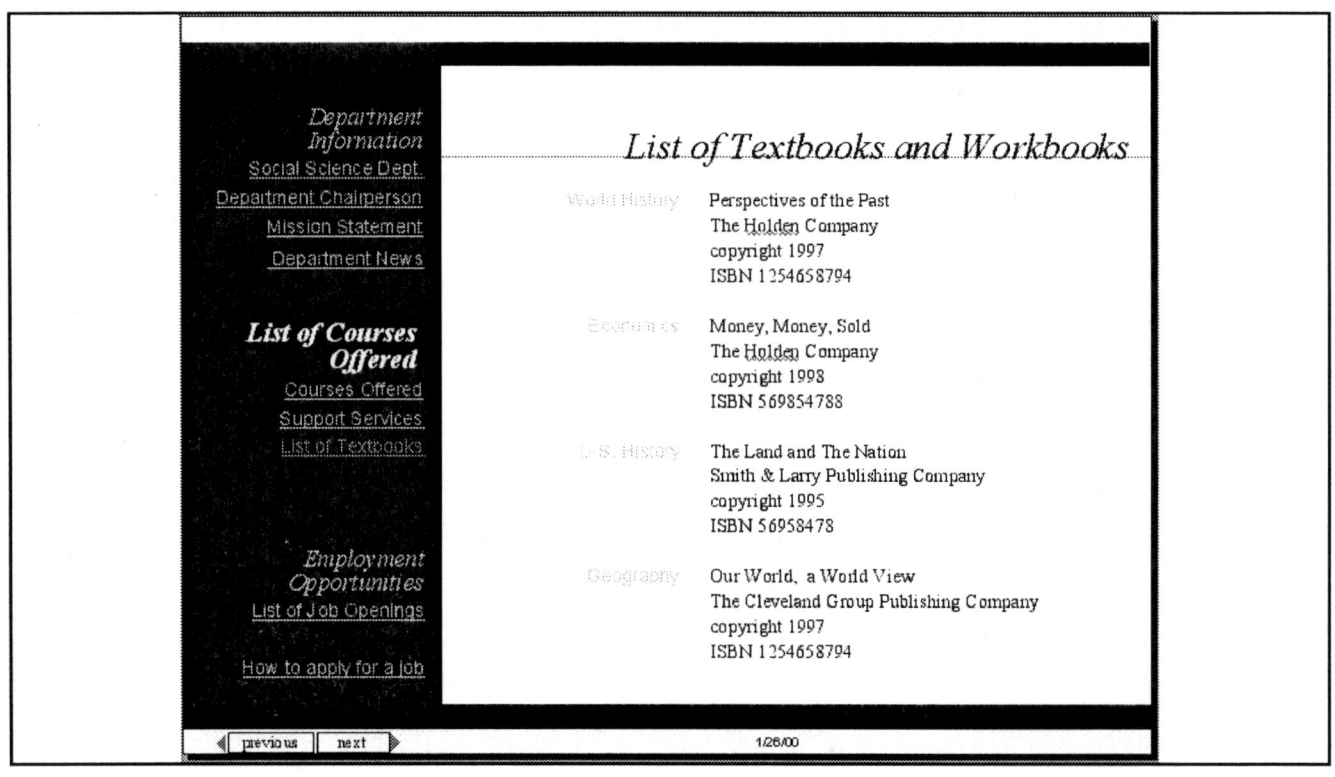

Social Studies

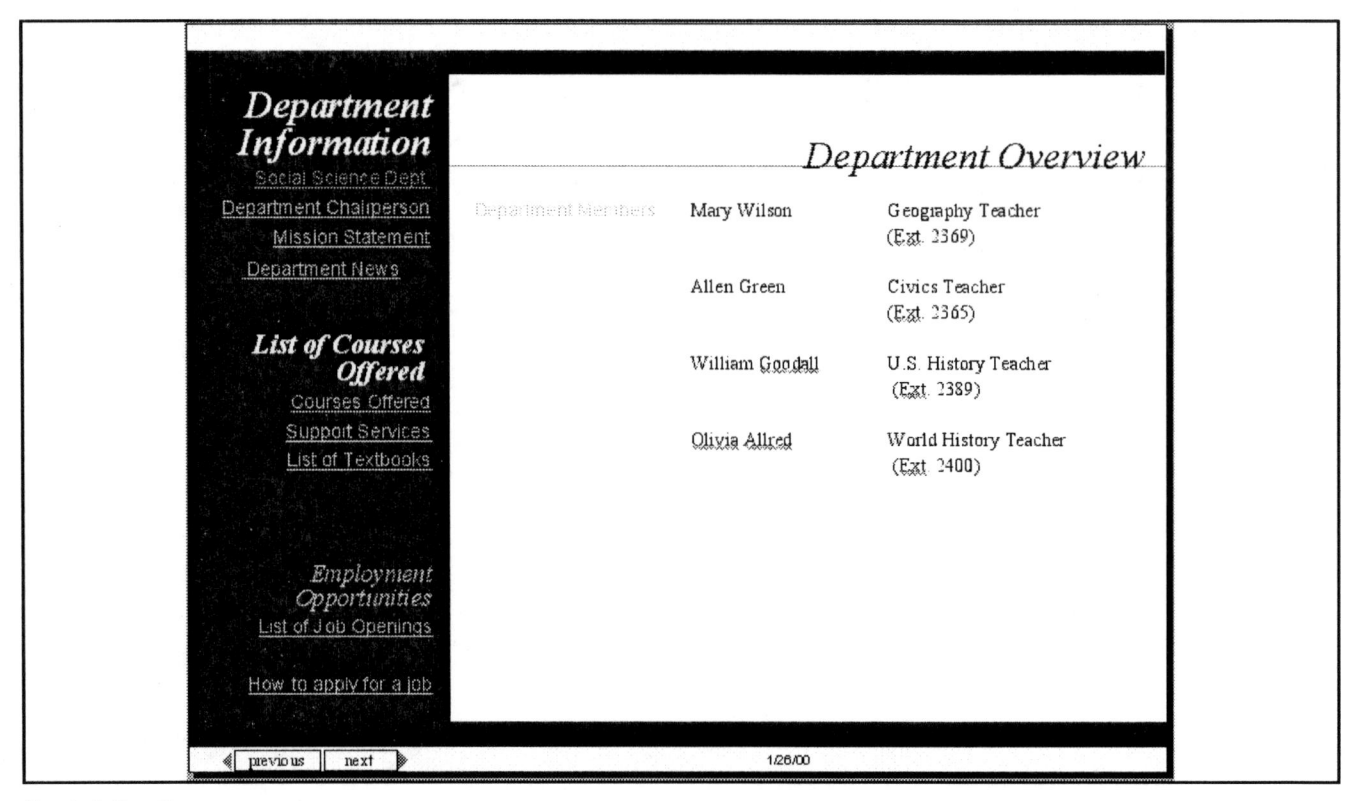

Social Studies

#2771 Teachers' Template Collection for Microsoft Office   76   © Teacher Created Resources, Inc.

Student Templates for Microsoft PowerPoint

Student Presentation Templates

Family Tree Presentation

My Family Tree
David William Sanchez

- Family Summary
- Parent's History
- Kid's History
- Grandparents
- Family Activities

Family Tree Opening Screen (Template File Name: Family Tree.pot)

Student Templates for Microsoft PowerPoint

Student Presentation Templates *(cont.)*

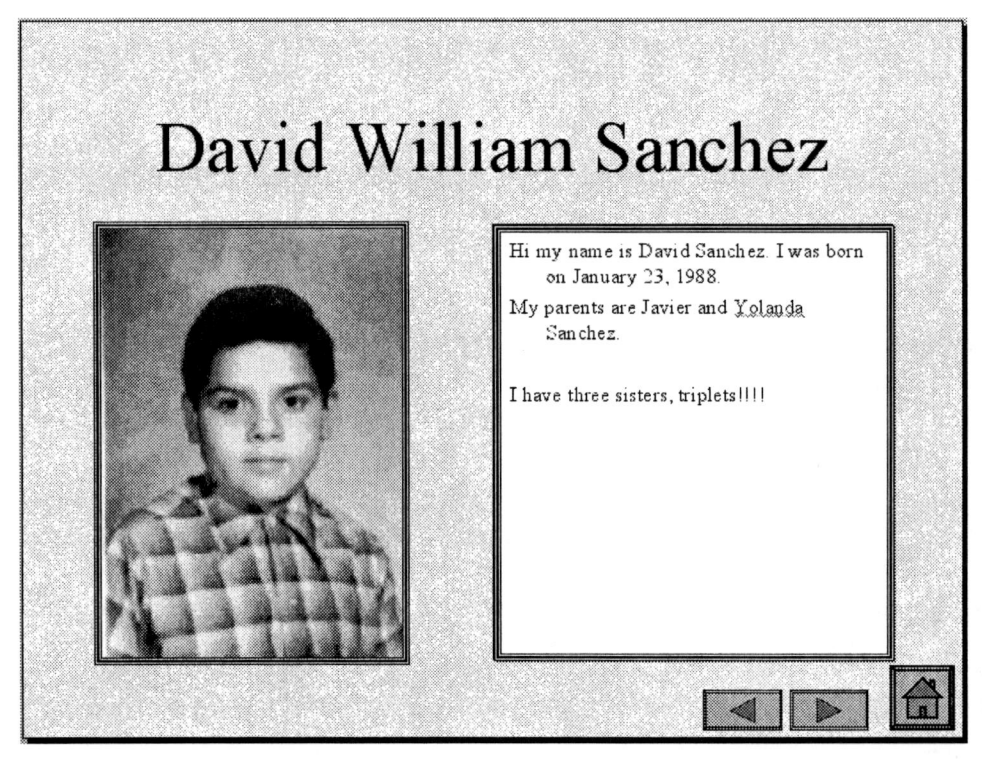

Family Tree Sample Screen

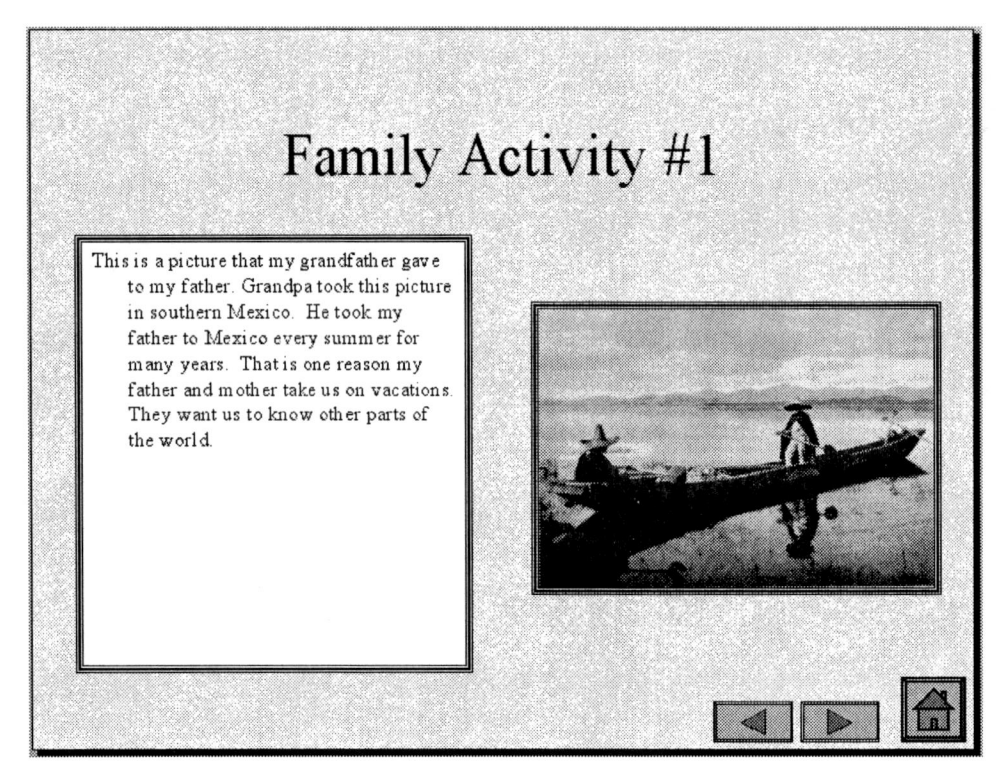

Family Tree Sample Screen

#2771 Teachers' Template Collection for Microsoft Office   78   © Teacher Created Resources, Inc.

Student Templates for Microsoft PowerPoint

Student Presentation Templates (cont.)

A Day at the Zoo Presentation

A Day at the Zoo (Opening Screen. Template File Name: A Day at the Zoo.pot)

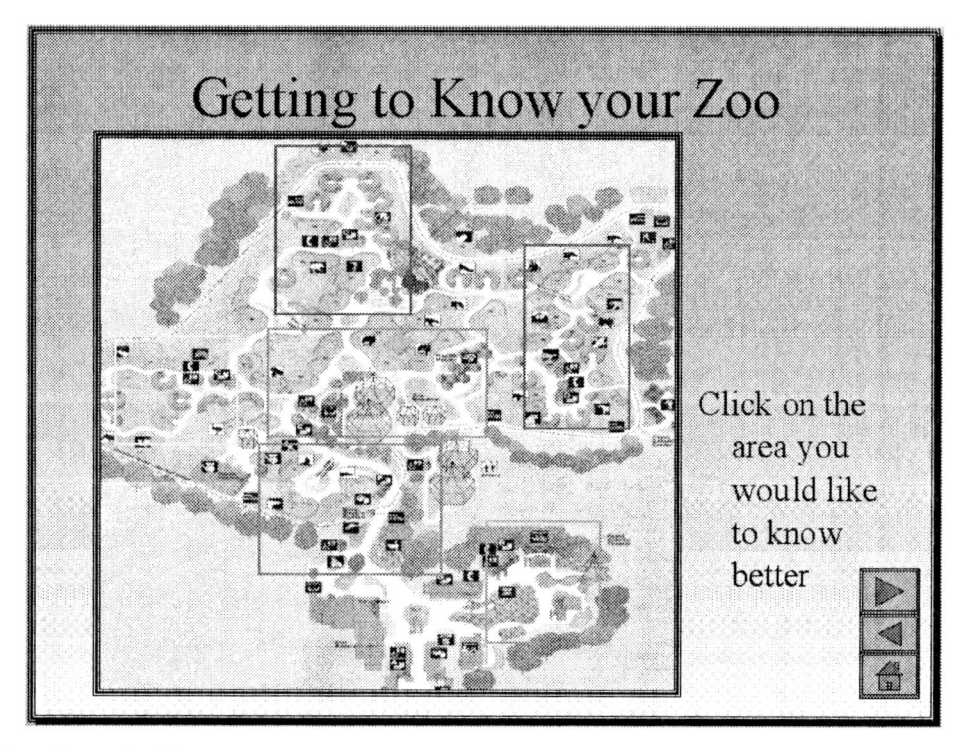

A Day at the Zoo Sample Screen

© *Teacher Created Resources, Inc.* 79 *#2771 Teachers' Template Collection for Microsoft Office*

Student Templates for Microsoft PowerPoint

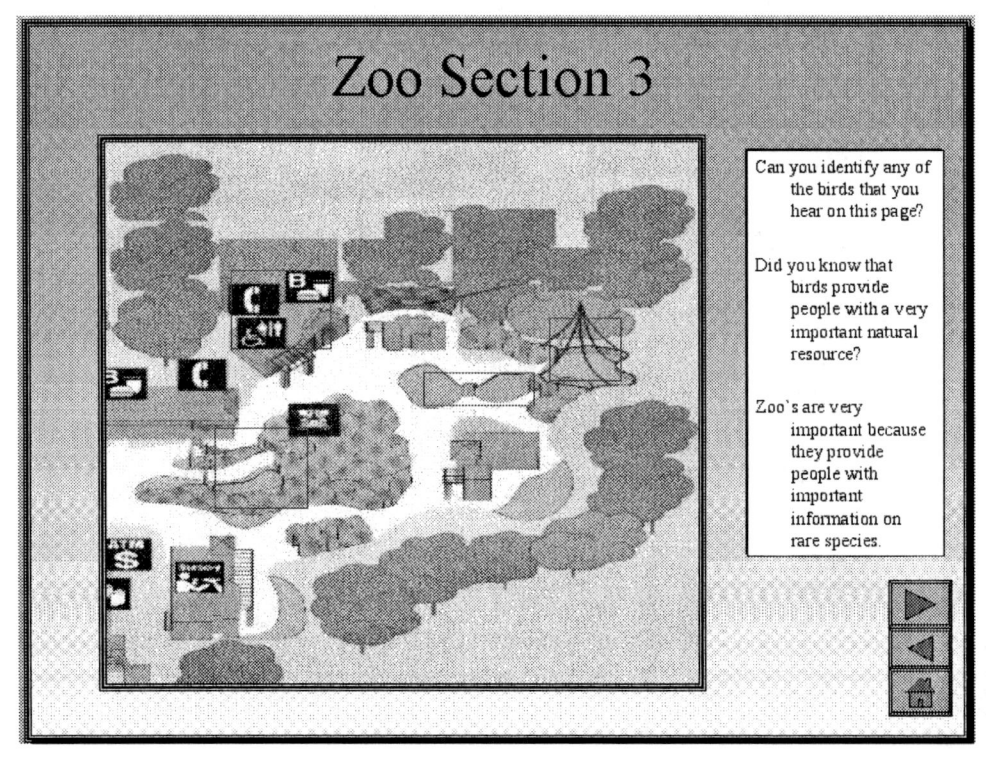

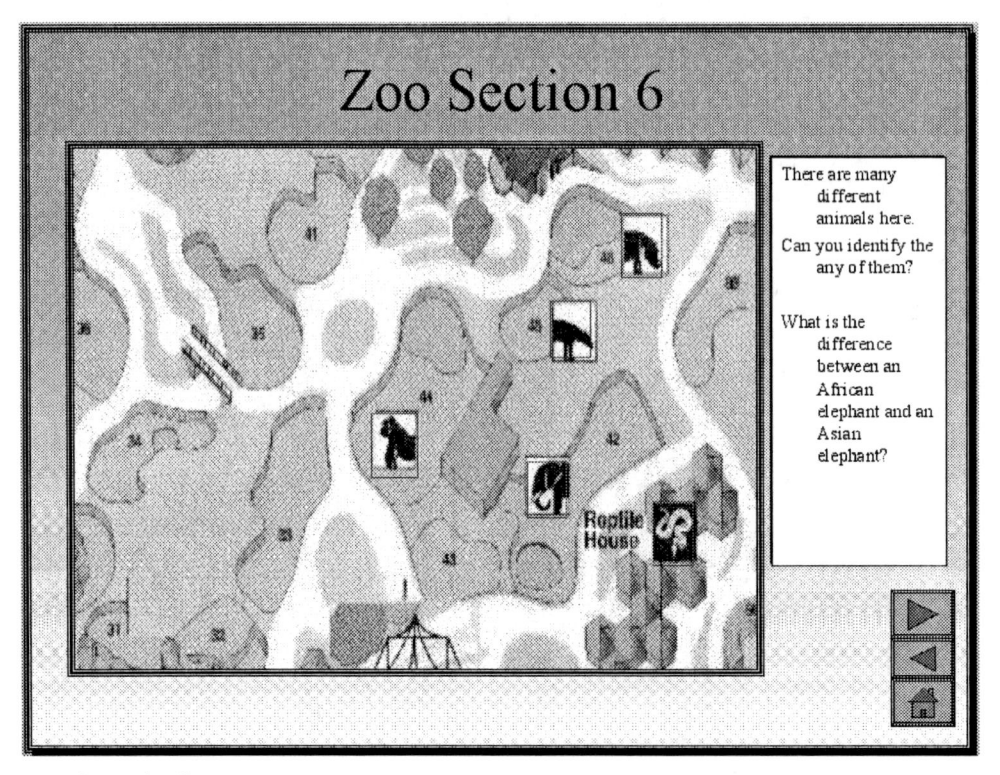

Student Presentation Templates *(cont.)*

A Day at the Zoo Sample Screen

A Day at the Zoo Sample Screen

Student Templates for Microsoft PowerPoint

Student Presentation Templates *(cont.)*

Storybook Maker Presentation

Storybook Maker (Template File Name: Story Book Maker.pot)

Student Templates for Microsoft PowerPoint

Student Presentation Templates *(cont.)*

Storybook Maker Sample Screen

Storybook Maker Sample Screen

Student Templates for Microsoft PowerPoint

Student Presentation Templates *(cont.)*

Study Guide Presentation

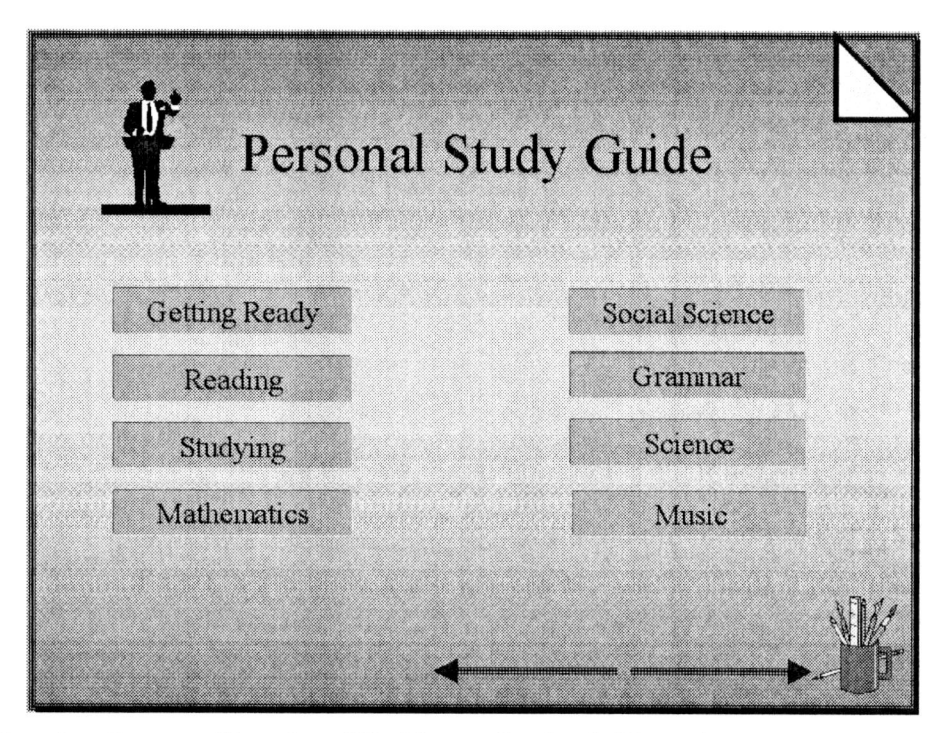

Study Guide (Opening Screen. Template File Name: Study Guide.pot)

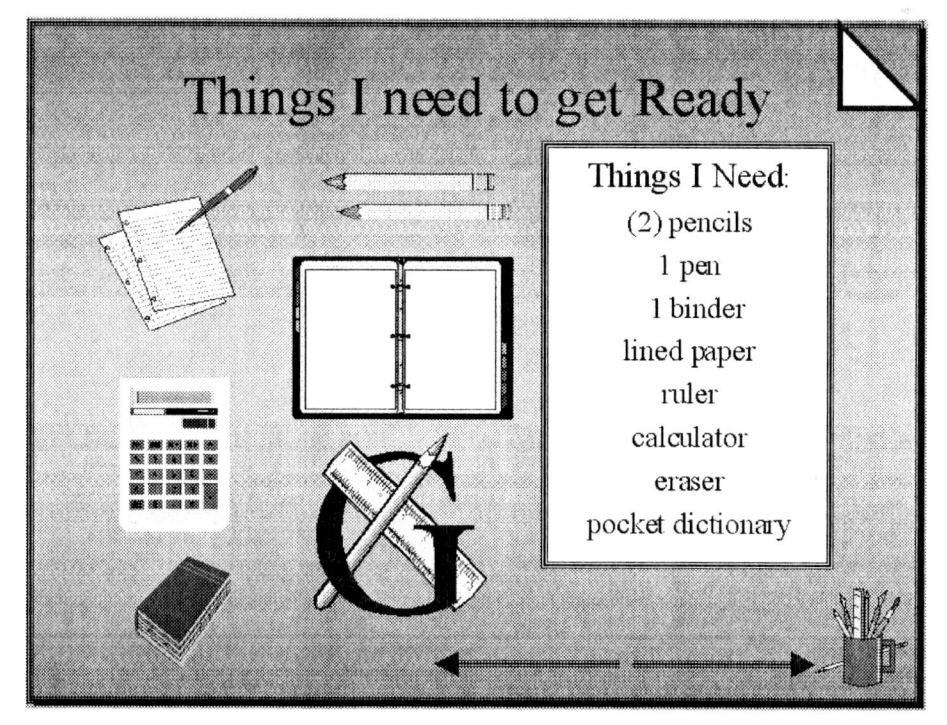

Study Guide Sample Screen

© *Teacher Created Resources, Inc.* 83 #2771 *Teachers' Template Collection for Microsoft Office*

Student Templates for Microsoft PowerPoint

Student Presentation Templates *(cont.)*

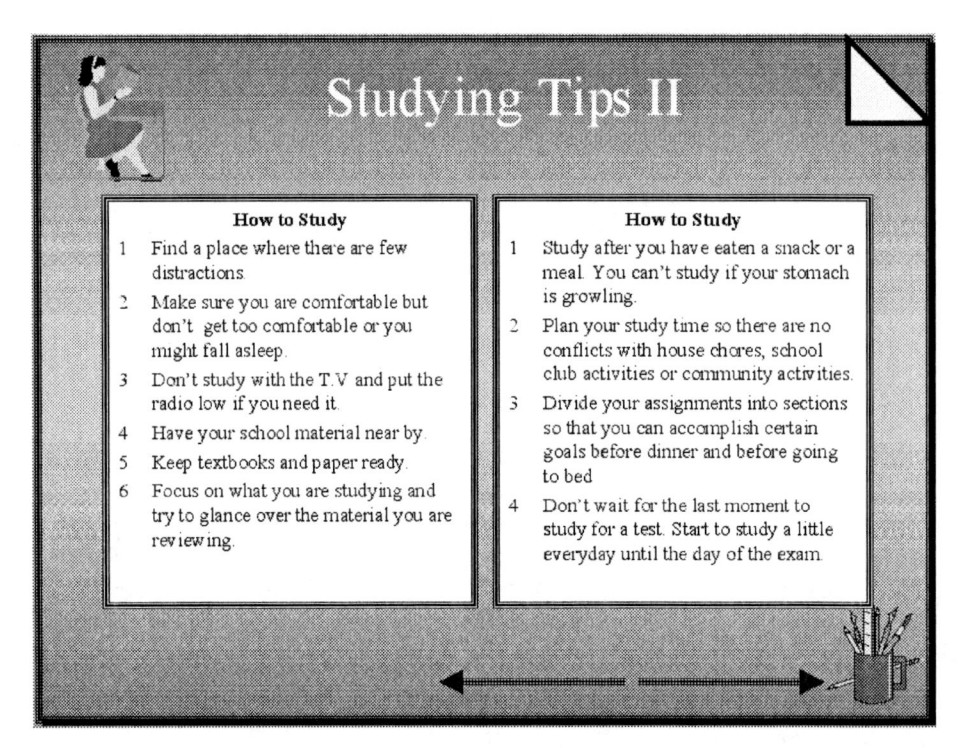

Study Guide Sample Screen

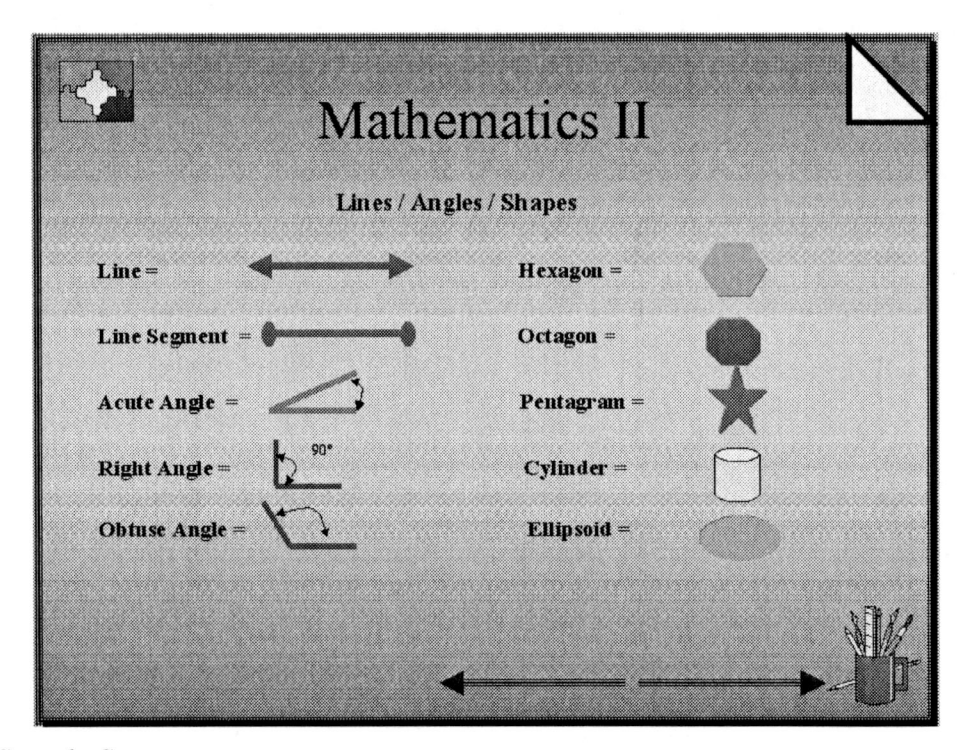

Study Guide Sample Screen

#2771 Teachers' Template Collection for Microsoft Office © Teacher Created Resources, Inc.

Student Templates for Microsoft PowerPoint

Student Presentation Templates *(cont.)*

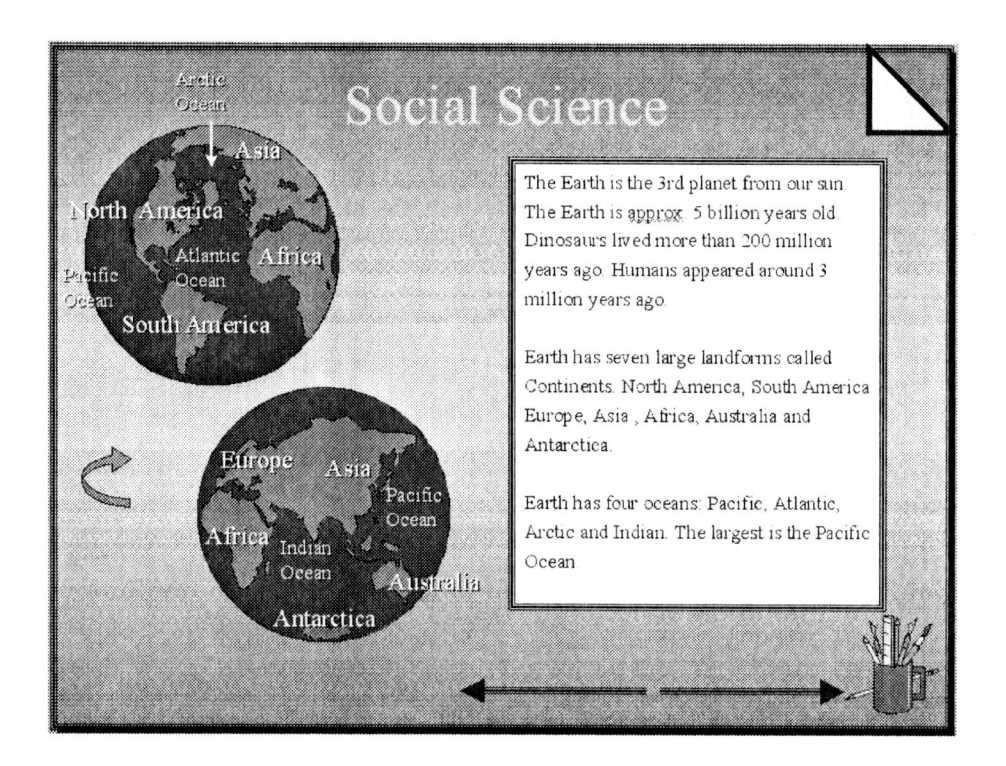

Social Science

The Earth is the 3rd planet from our sun. The Earth is approx. 5 billion years old. Dinosaurs lived more than 200 million years ago. Humans appeared around 3 million years ago.

Earth has seven large landforms called Continents. North America, South America Europe, Asia, Africa, Australia and Antarctica.

Earth has four oceans: Pacific, Atlantic, Arctic and Indian. The largest is the Pacific Ocean.

Study Guide

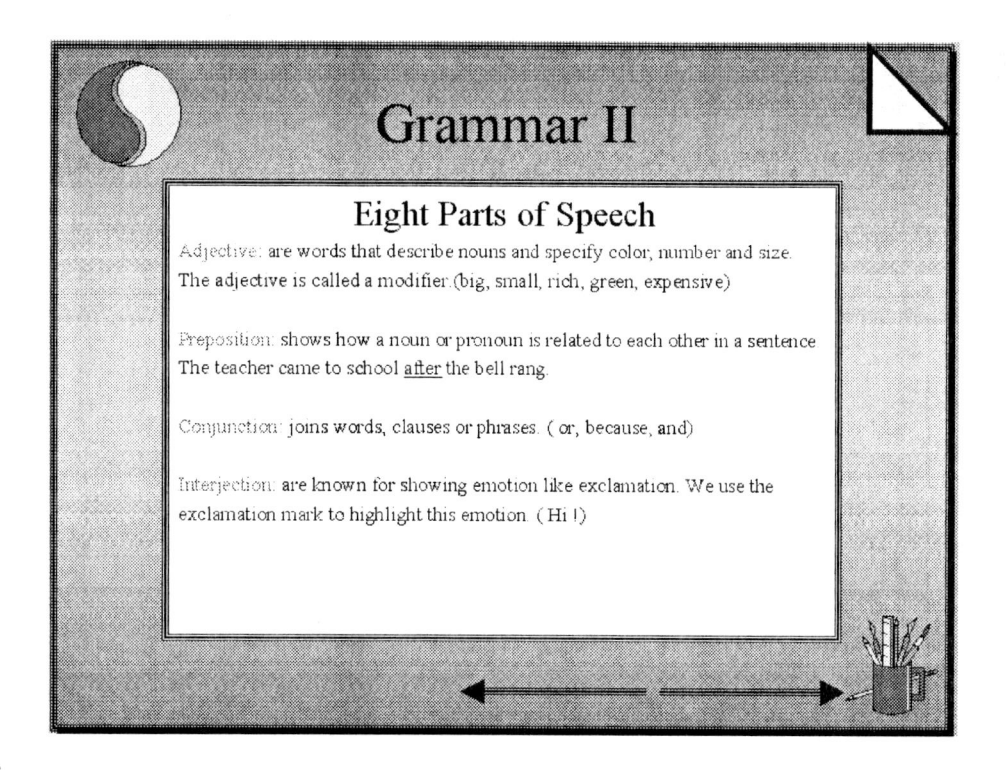

Grammar II

Eight Parts of Speech

Adjective: are words that describe nouns and specify color, number and size. The adjective is called a modifier.(big, small, rich, green, expensive)

Preposition: shows how a noun or pronoun is related to each other in a sentence The teacher came to school after the bell rang.

Conjunction: joins words, clauses or phrases. (or, because, and)

Interjection: are known for showing emotion like exclamation. We use the exclamation mark to highlight this emotion. (Hi !)

Study Guide

© *Teacher Created Resources, Inc.* 85 #2771 *Teachers' Template Collection for Microsoft Office*

Student Templates for Microsoft PowerPoint

Student Presentation Templates *(cont.)*

Electronic Yearbook Presentation

Electronic Yearbook (Opening Screen. Template File Name: The Electronic Yearbook.pot)

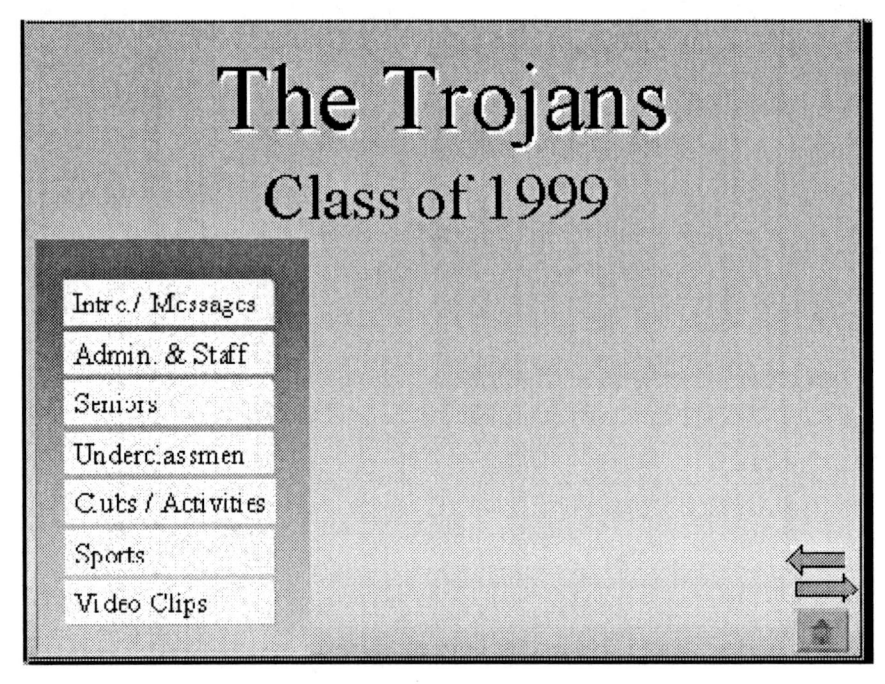

Electronic Yearbook Sample Screen

#2771 *Teachers' Template Collection for Microsoft Office*   86   © *Teacher Created Resources, Inc.*

Student Templates for Microsoft PowerPoint

Student Presentation Templates *(cont.)*

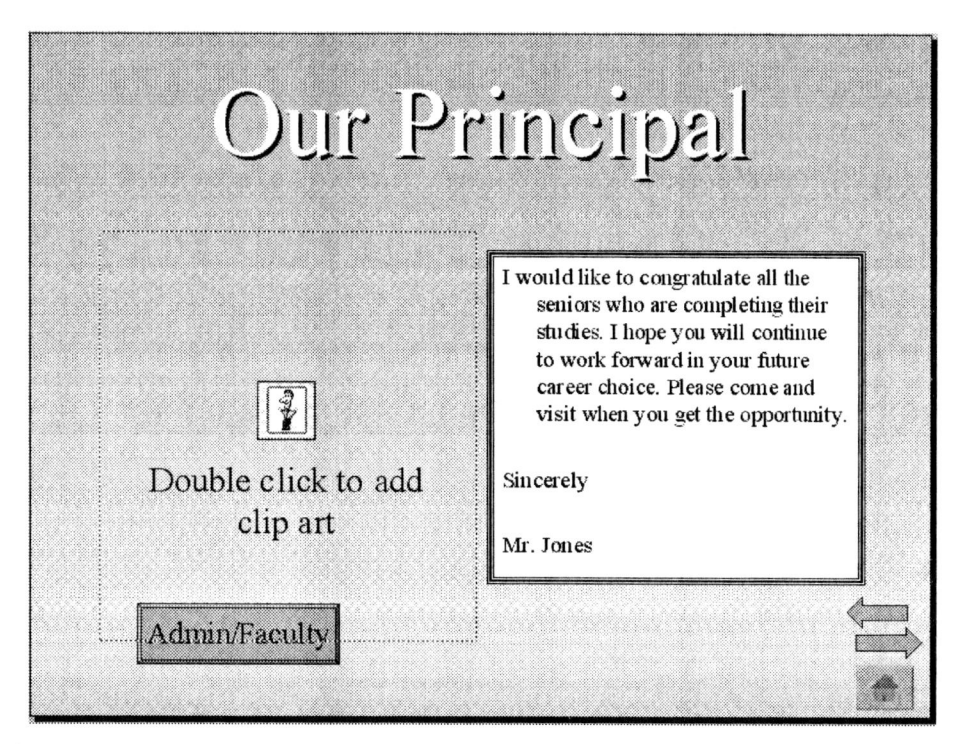

Electronic Yearbook Sample Screen

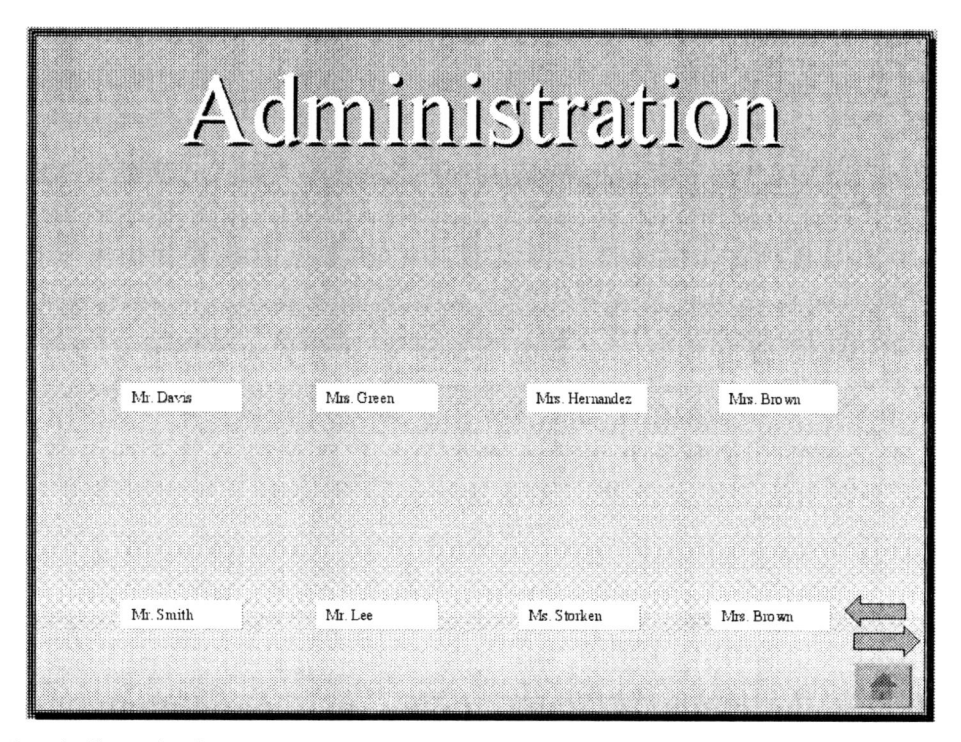

Electronic Yearbook Sample Screen

© *Teacher Created Resources, Inc.* 87 *#2771 Teachers' Template Collection for Microsoft Office*

Student Templates for Microsoft PowerPoint

Student Presentation Templates *(cont.)*

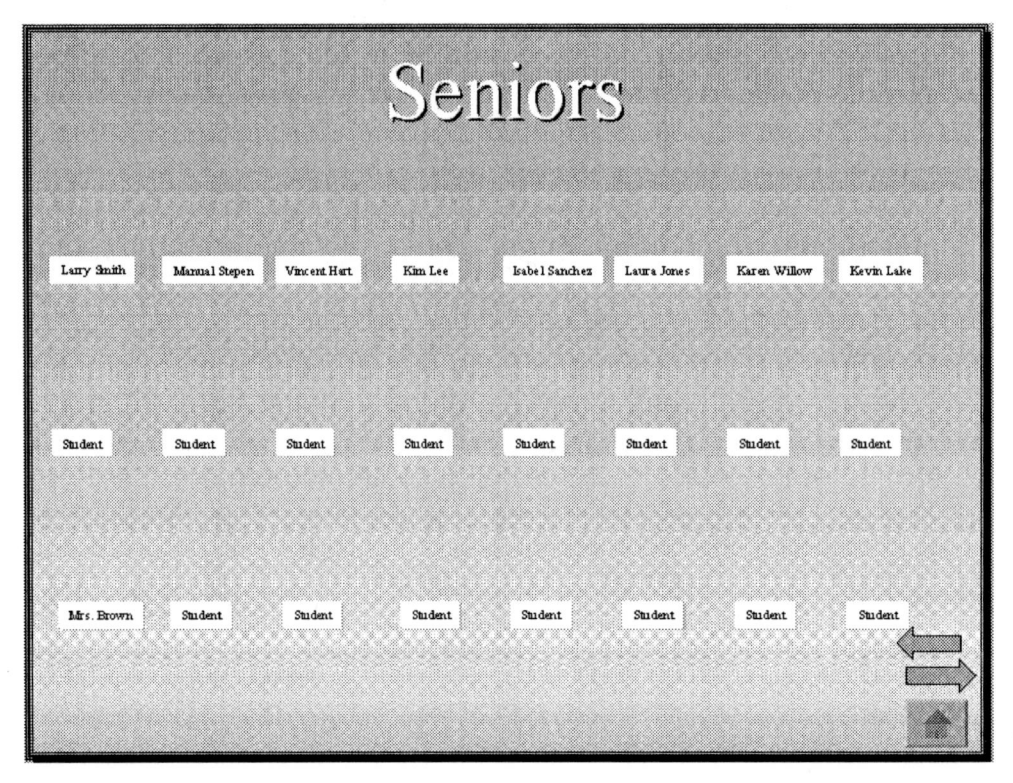

Electronic Yearbook

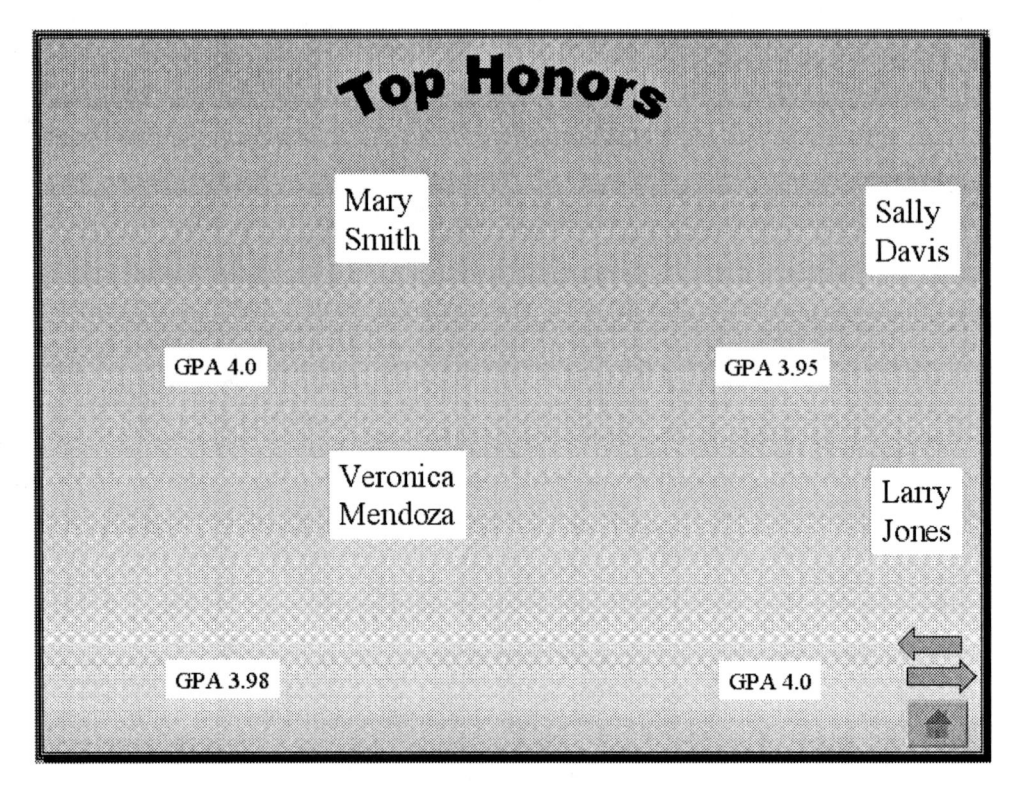

Electronic Yearbook

Student Templates for Microsoft PowerPoint

Student Presentation Templates *(cont.)*

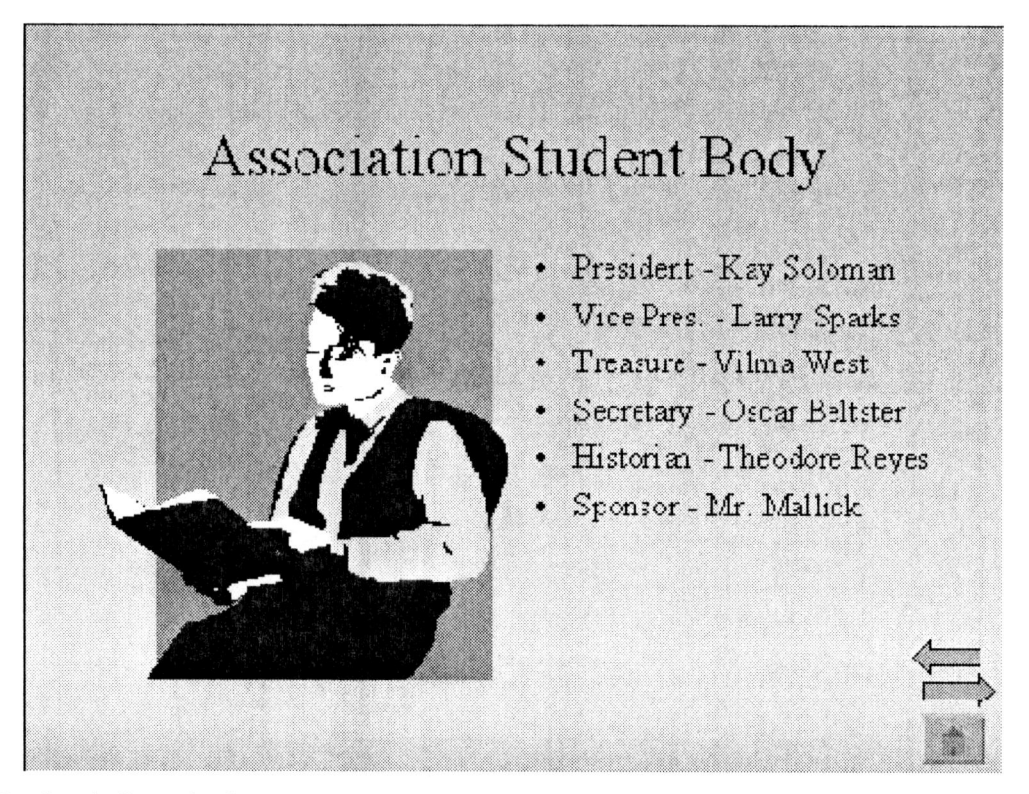

Electronic Yearbook Sample Screen

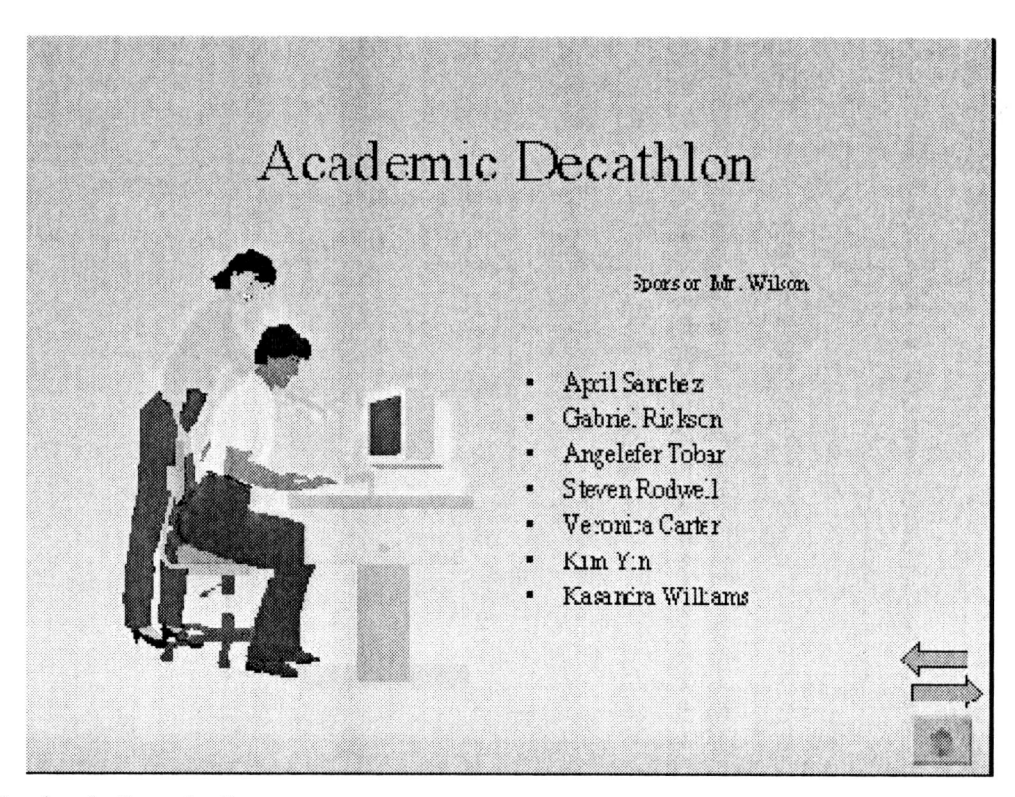

Electronic Yearbook Sample Screen

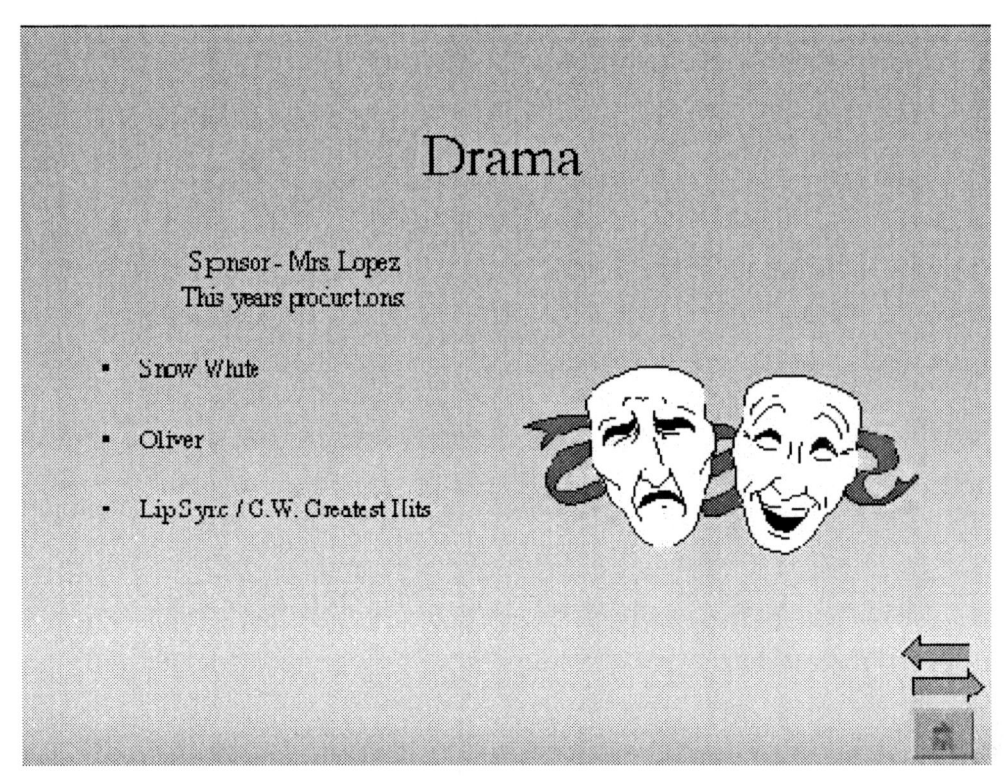

Student Templates for Microsoft PowerPoint

Student Presentation Templates *(cont.)*

Electronic Yearbook Sample Screen

Electronic Yearbook Sample Screen

Student Templates for Microsoft PowerPoint

Student Presentation Templates (cont.)

Electronic Yearbook Sample Screen

Electronic Yearbook Sample Screen

© *Teacher Created Resources, Inc.* 91 *#2771 Teachers' Template Collection for Microsoft Office*

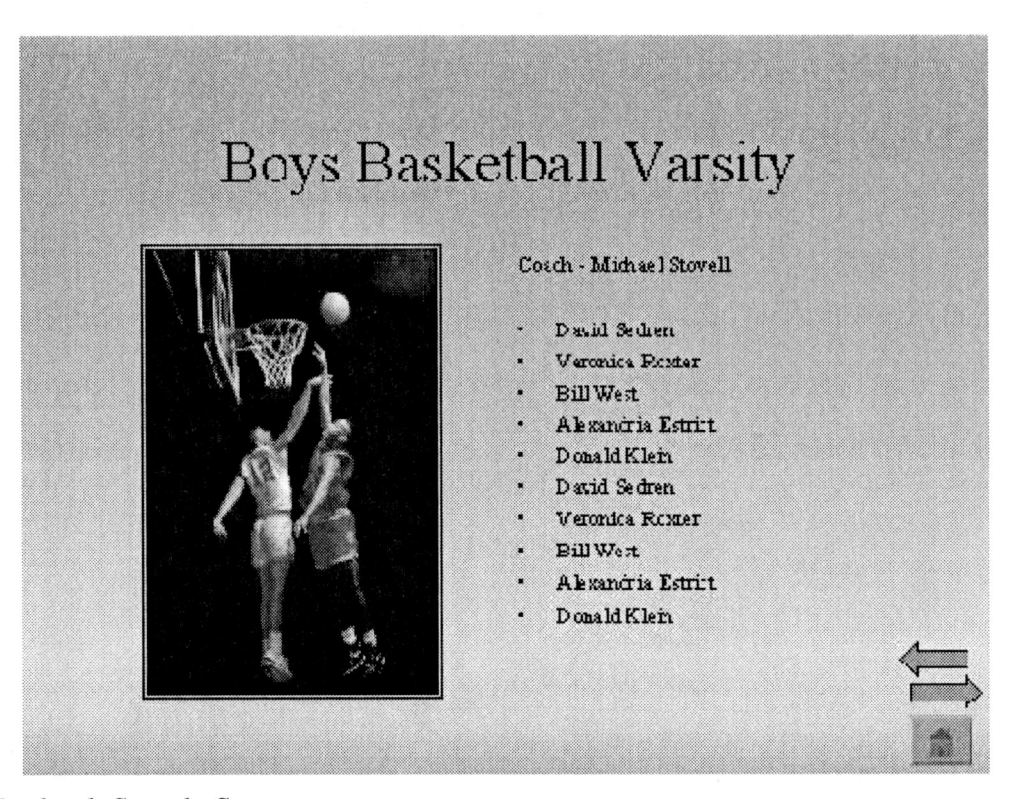

Student Templates for Microsoft PowerPoint

Student Presentation Templates *(cont.)*

Electronic Yearbook Sample Screen

Electronic Yearbook Sample Screen

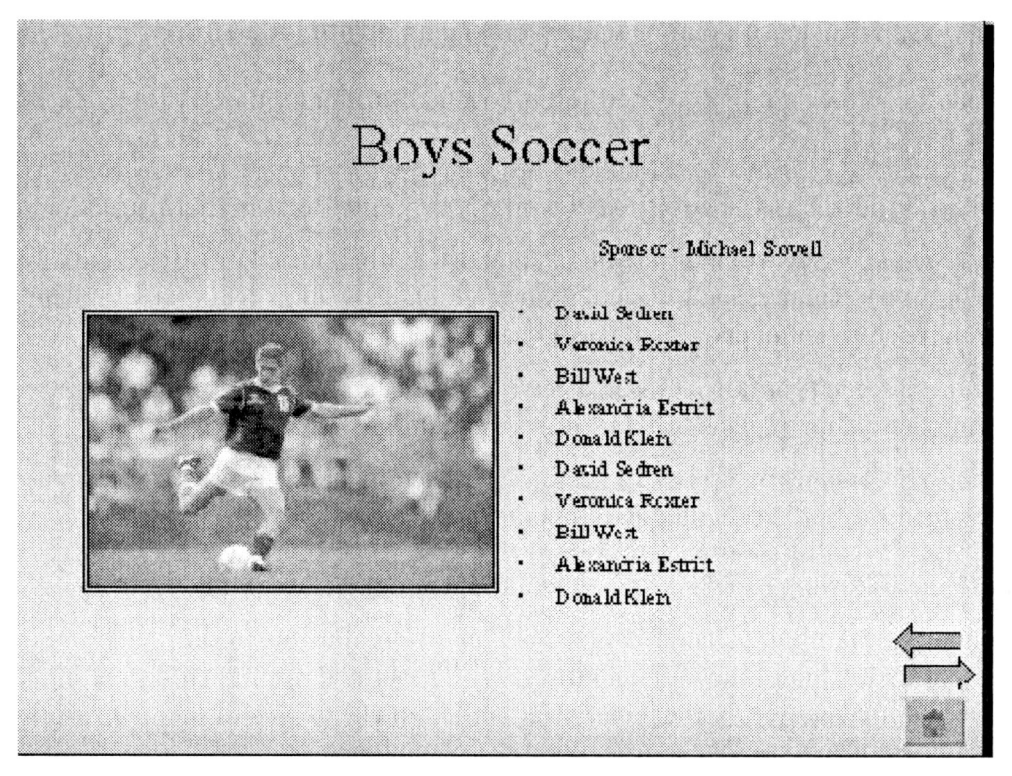

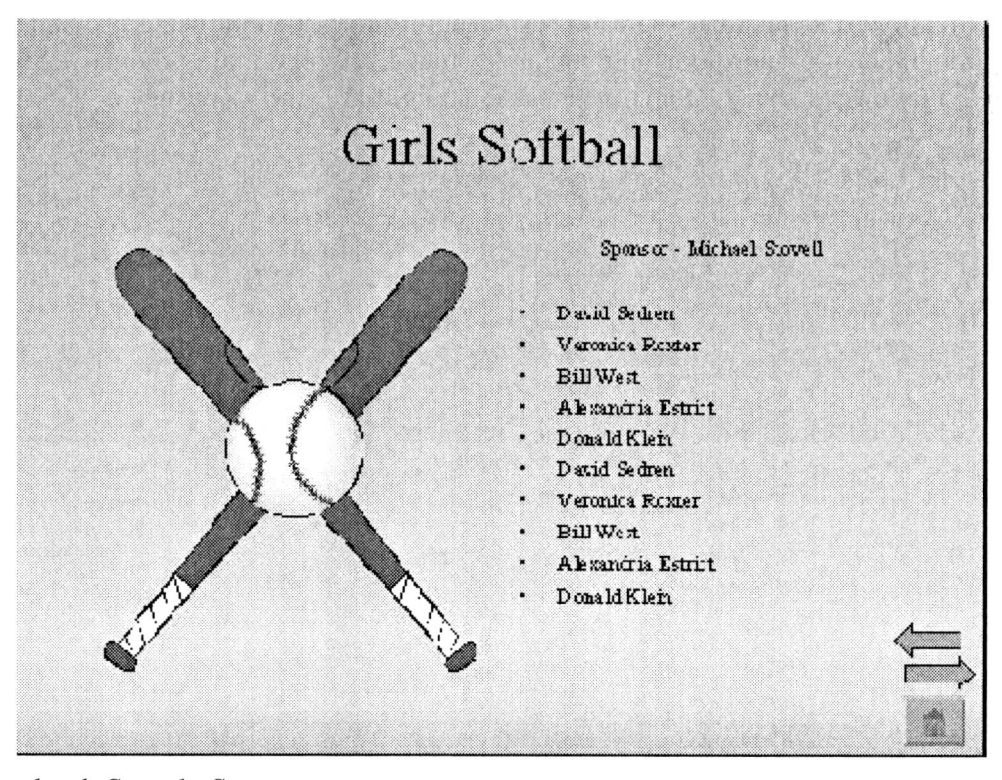

Student Templates for Microsoft PowerPoint

Student Presentation Templates *(cont.)*

Electronic Yearbook Sample Screen

Electronic Yearbook Sample Screen

© *Teacher Created Resources, Inc.* 93 *#2771 Teachers' Template Collection for Microsoft Office*

Teacher Templates for Microsoft Excel

The *Microsoft Excel* templates contain workbooks for teachers and students. The workbooks are designed for immediate use and can be edited to meet your personal needs. These templates are designed to help teachers manage grading and lesson planning with little effort.

The math templates can be altered to meet different levels of difficulty based on grade level or student proficiency.

Teachers can use the following *Microsoft Excel* workbooks in their classroom instruction:

- *Grade Book Deluxe:* a working grade book spreadsheet that automatically calculates grades, student scoring percentage, and a visual grading graph, as well as listing assignments by period for easy reference for students. Each period can contain up to 75 students.
- *Lesson Plan:* designed for 20-week semesters, teachers can organize their daily or weekly lesson plans. Printouts facilitate plans for substitutes and administrators.
- *Seating Charts:* contains two styles of seating charts contained in worksheet formats that facilitate the management of student seating assignments.

Students can use the following *Microsoft Excel* workbooks in the classroom:

- *Math:* contains working models of math, based on different levels of difficulty and includes addition, subtraction, multiplication and division. These models are self-correcting and will give final scores automatically. Teachers can print out and make copies of the math worksheets or students can complete worksheets directly on the computer.
- *Student Planner:* allows students to design a personalized education plan, keep track of homework assignments with better planning and organization through the use of technology. This electronic planner will allow students to take greater responsibility for scheduling and managing their school week. Through better organization and planning, students will be more productive at school. This program will allow students to demonstrate accountability for the work they do at school.

Teacher Templates for Microsoft Excel

Teacher Templates

The Grade Book

To use Grade Book complete the following steps:

1. Open the Grade Book template.
2. Click to select the key fields and replace them with your information (school name, teacher name, class name, section number, student names, and school identification number).
3. Beginning in cell J, enter the name of the assignment.
4. Beginning in cell J4, type the date of the assignment (9/23/99) and the date will automatically be converted into the day and month (23 Sept).
5. Beginning in cell J6, enter the value of the assignment (points).

The grading scale is located in cell A99.

Note: Certain columns contain formulas that will be lost if the cell is highlighted and deleted. Type over the existing data and clear areas that you will not use. Remember you can always copy a cell formula and paste it on the cell where a formula is missing.

	A	B	C	D	E	F	G	H	I	J	K	L	M	N	O	P
1		George Washington High School				Video Technology				Video Tips Xerox	TV Viewing Habits	Storybrd Puppet Show	Puppet Workshop	TV Viewing Habits	VCR Tape Favorite Prog.	Xword Puzzle
2		GRADE BOOK/CLASS ROSTER				PERIOD 1		YEAR: 98-99								
3		ALEJANDRA MARTINEZ				SECTION: 118		COURSE: 5581								
4										15-Sep	17-Sep	21-Sep	21-Sep	10-Sep	22-Sep	21-Se
5		CLASS	LAST NAME	FIRST NAME	STUDENT ID	FINAL GRADE	PERCENT GRADE	TOTAL POINTS								
6				MAXIMUM POSSIBLE--->				166		5	5	10	20	5	10	10
7	1	12	Benavidez	Monique	266	B	82.53%	137		5	5	7	15	5	10	10
8	2	12	Calderon	Claudia	0349	B	87.35%	145		0	5	10	15	5	0	10
9	3	11	Contreras	Marcelo	0532	A	99.40%	165		5	5	10	20	5	10	10
10	4	12	Flores	Claudia	4186	A	98.19%	163		5	5	8	20	5	10	10
11	5	11	Gomez	Antonio	940	F	9.04%	15		5	0	0	0	0	0	0
12	6	11	Gomez	Genaro	949	D	66.27%	110		5	5	10	20	5	10	10
13	7	12	Hernandez	Eddie	1096	A	93.37%	155		5	5	10	20	5	0	10
14	8	11	Lopez	Ramon	1355	F	46.99%	78		5	4	10	0	4	0	10
15	9	12	Macias	Alejandra	1389	B	84.34%	140		5	5	10	15	5	10	10
16	10	12	Martinez	Ivan	1463	B	87.35%	145		5	5	5	15	5	0	10
17	11	11	Melendez	Efren	1527	F	7.83%	13		5	0	8	0	0	0	0
18	12	11	Mendoza	Maria	1542	A	93.37%	155		5	5	10	20	5	10	10
19	13	11	Mojica	Jose	1581	NM	0.00%	0		0	0	0	0	0	0	0
20	14	11	Morales	Elizabeth	1611	B	89.16%	148		5	5	8	15	5	10	10
21	15	10	Naborne	Michael	1676	A	93.37%	155		5	5	10	20	5	10	10
22	16	12	Ochoa	Jose	1751	A	93.37%	155		5	5	5	15	5	10	10
23	17	12	Perez	Rolando	4250	A	93.37%	155		5	5	10	15	10	10	10
24	18	11	Thompson	Jeffery	2477	A	100.00%	166		5	8	8	20	5	10	10
25	19	12	Foncerrada	Jose	4361	B	87.35%	145		0	5	10	20	0	0	10
26	20	12	Gonzalez	Esmeralda	0963	C	78.31%	130		5	5	10	20	10	0	0
27	21	11	Arresis	Enrique	161	C	75.30%	125		0	0	15	0	0	0	10

Grade Book Main Screen (Template File Name: Grade Book Deluxe.xlt)

Teacher Templates for Microsoft Excel

Teacher Templates *(cont.)*

The Grade Book *(cont.)*

The program will automatically calculate grades and total points for the teacher. Teachers can arrange grading scales and percentages for final grades. Teachers can also create additional assignments for extra credit work. They can set the print screen area in order to print only student ID numbers and their scores. The Assignment screen can be printed to help students identify missing assignments.

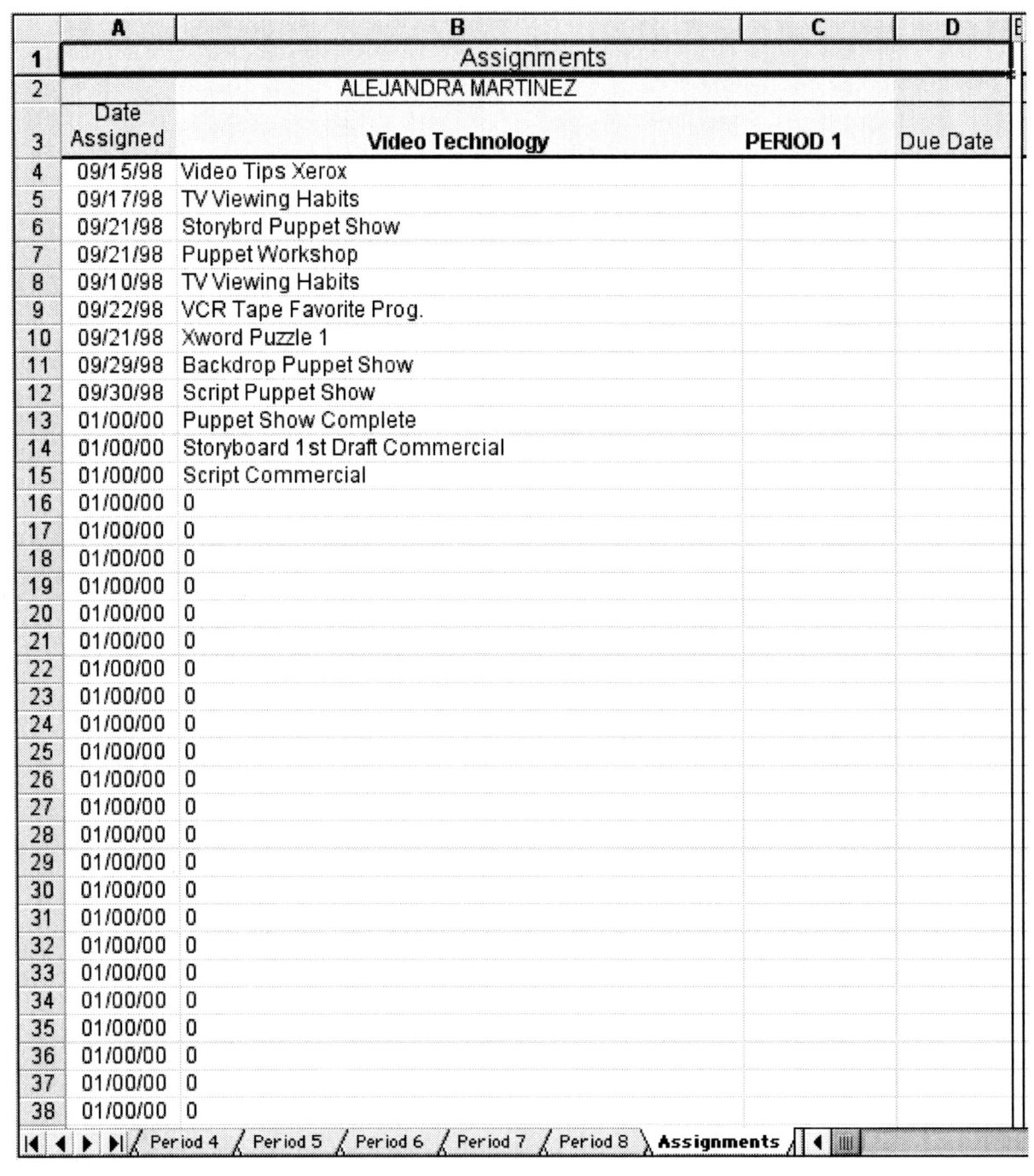

	A	B	C	D
1		Assignments		
2		ALEJANDRA MARTINEZ		
3	Date Assigned	Video Technology	PERIOD 1	Due Date
4	09/15/98	Video Tips Xerox		
5	09/17/98	TV Viewing Habits		
6	09/21/98	Storybrd Puppet Show		
7	09/21/98	Puppet Workshop		
8	09/10/98	TV Viewing Habits		
9	09/22/98	VCR Tape Favorite Prog.		
10	09/21/98	Xword Puzzle 1		
11	09/29/98	Backdrop Puppet Show		
12	09/30/98	Script Puppet Show		
13	01/00/00	Puppet Show Complete		
14	01/00/00	Storyboard 1st Draft Commercial		
15	01/00/00	Script Commercial		
16	01/00/00	0		
17	01/00/00	0		
18	01/00/00	0		
19	01/00/00	0		
20	01/00/00	0		
21	01/00/00	0		
22	01/00/00	0		
23	01/00/00	0		
24	01/00/00	0		
25	01/00/00	0		
26	01/00/00	0		
27	01/00/00	0		
28	01/00/00	0		
29	01/00/00	0		
30	01/00/00	0		
31	01/00/00	0		
32	01/00/00	0		
33	01/00/00	0		
34	01/00/00	0		
35	01/00/00	0		
36	01/00/00	0		
37	01/00/00	0		
38	01/00/00	0		

Period 4 / Period 5 / Period 6 / Period 7 / Period 8 \ Assignments

Grade Book Assignment Sample Screen

Teacher Templates for Microsoft Excel

Teacher Templates *(cont.)*

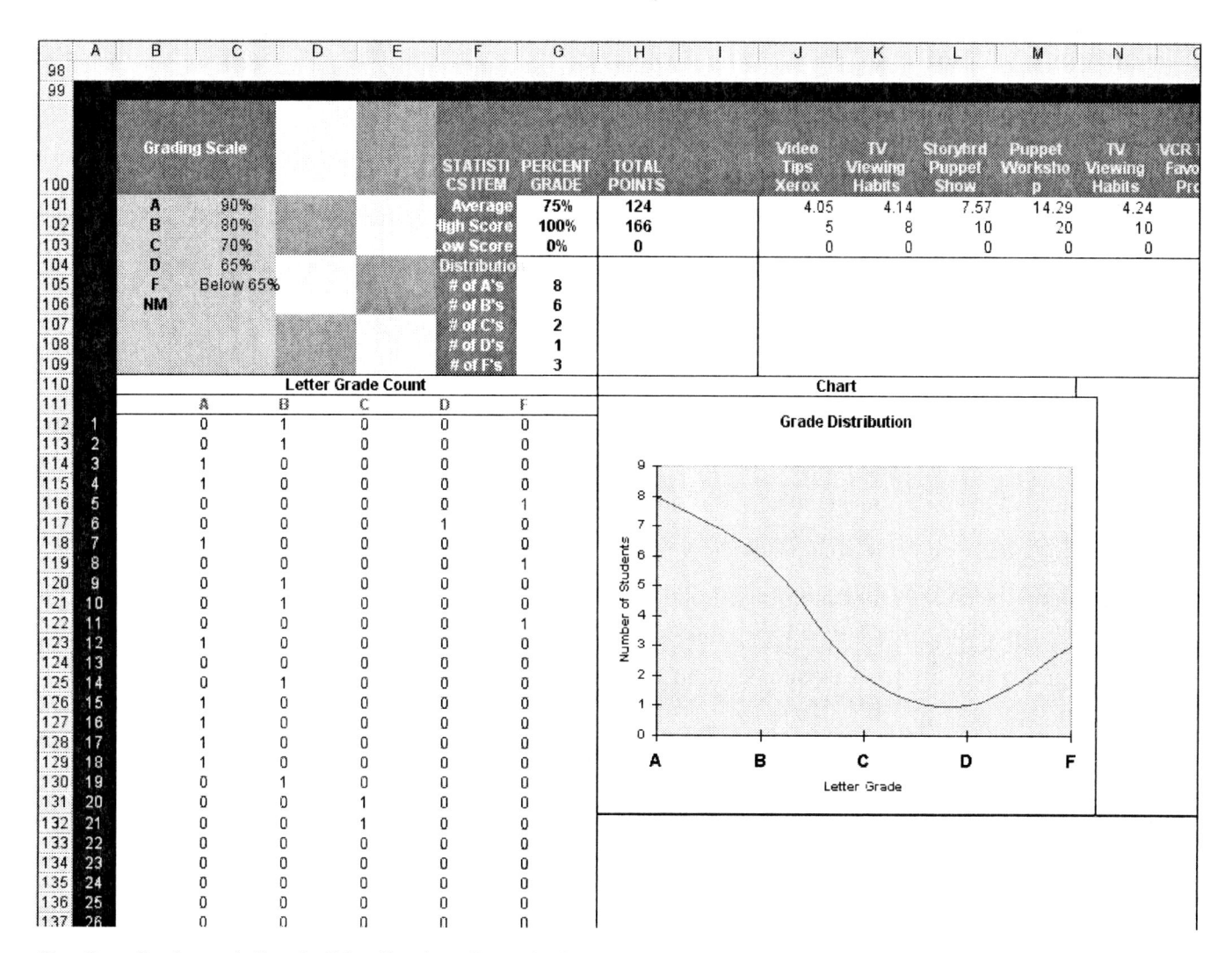

	A	B	C	D	E	F	G	H	I	J	K	L	M	N
98														
99														
100		Grading Scale				STATISTICS ITEM	PERCENT GRADE	TOTAL POINTS		Video Tips Xerox	TV Viewing Habits	Storybrd Puppet Show	Puppet Workshop	TV Viewing Habits	VCR Favo Pr
101		A	90%			Average	75%	124		4.05	4.14	7.57	14.29	4.24
102		B	80%			High Score	100%	166		5	8	10	20	10
103		C	70%			Low Score	0%	0		0	0	0	0	0
104		D	65%			Distribution								
105		F	Below 65%			# of A's	8							
106		NM				# of B's	6							
107						# of C's	2							
108						# of D's	1							
109						# of F's	3							
110				Letter Grade Count							Chart			
111			A	B	C	D	F							
112	1		0	1	0	0	0							
113	2		0	1	0	0	0							
114	3		1	0	0	0	0							
115	4		1	0	0	0	0							
116	5		0	0	0	0	1							
117	6		0	0	0	1	0							
118	7		1	0	0	0	0							
119	8		0	0	0	0	1							
120	9		0	1	0	0	0							
121	10		0	1	0	0	0							
122	11		0	0	0	0	1							
123	12		1	0	0	0	0							
124	13		0	0	0	0	0							
125	14		0	1	0	0	0							
126	15		1	0	0	0	0							
127	16		1	0	0	0	0							
128	17		1	0	0	0	0							
129	18		1	0	0	0	0							
130	19		0	1	0	0	0							
131	20		0	0	1	0	0							
132	21		0	0	1	0	0							
133	22		0	0	0	0	0							
134	23		0	0	0	0	0							
135	24		0	0	0	0	0							
136	25		0	0	0	0	0							
137	26		0	0	0	0	0							

Grade Distribution chart showing Number of Students vs. Letter Grade (A through F).

Grading Scale and Grade Distribution Sample Screen

Teacher Templates for Microsoft Excel

Teacher Templates *(cont.)*

Lesson Plan Spreadsheet

The Lesson Plan Spreadsheet is organized into twenty one-week spreadsheets. Each week is organized into a Monday through Friday schedule. Teachers can organize a semester's worth of lessons and then create a new template workbook for the second semester. They can also change the number of spreadsheets to fit into a quarterly system. Printouts can provide information for substitutes and administrators.

To modify the Lesson Plan Spreadsheet, complete the following steps:

1. Go to cell K1 and enter the date (number) for Monday of the first week of the semester. The spreadsheet will automatically arrange the remaining 20 weeks of the semester.

2. Go to cell K2 and enter the semester year, and the program will apply that information to the rest of the spreadsheet.

3. Click in cell C2 and enter the teacher's name and cell C3 to enter the school's name.

4. Click in cell E3 and enter the academic year information.

5. Click in cell B6, C6, D6, E6, through I6 and enter the subject. The spreadsheet program will automatically apply that information throughout the worksheets.

6. Click in any day of the week and begin to enter your lesson plans.

Lesson Plan Spreadsheet (Template File Name: Lesson Planner.xlt)

Teacher Templates for Microsoft Excel

Teacher Templates (cont.)

Seating Charts

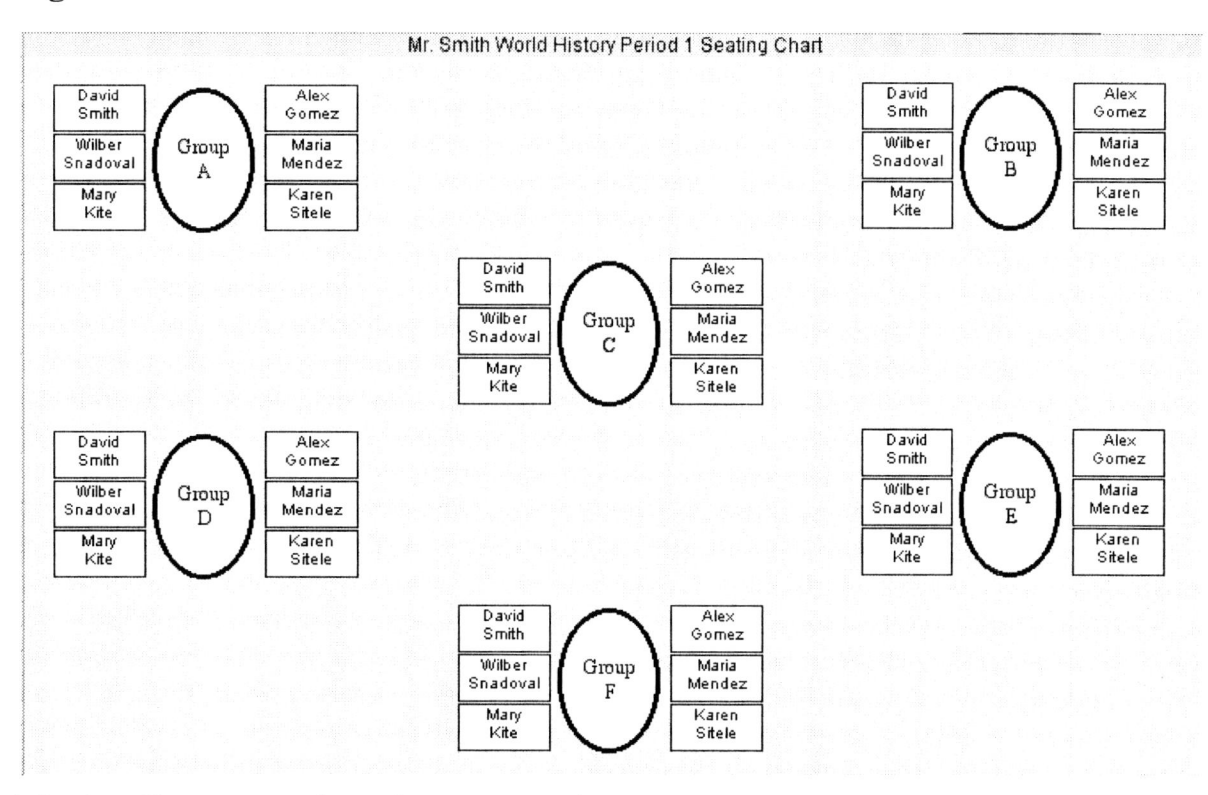

Mr. Smith World History Period 1 Seating Chart

Group A: David Smith, Wilber Snadoval, Mary Kite, Alex Gomez, Maria Mendez, Karen Sitele

Group B: David Smith, Wilber Snadoval, Mary Kite, Alex Gomez, Maria Mendez, Karen Sitele

Group C: David Smith, Wilber Snadoval, Mary Kite, Alex Gomez, Maria Mendez, Karen Sitele

Group D: David Smith, Wilber Snadoval, Mary Kite, Alex Gomez, Maria Mendez, Karen Sitele

Group E: David Smith, Wilber Snadoval, Mary Kite, Alex Gomez, Maria Mendez, Karen Sitele

Group F: David Smith, Wilber Snadoval, Mary Kite, Alex Gomez, Maria Mendez, Karen Sitele

Excel Seating Charts (Template File Name: Seating Chart Groups 1.xlt)

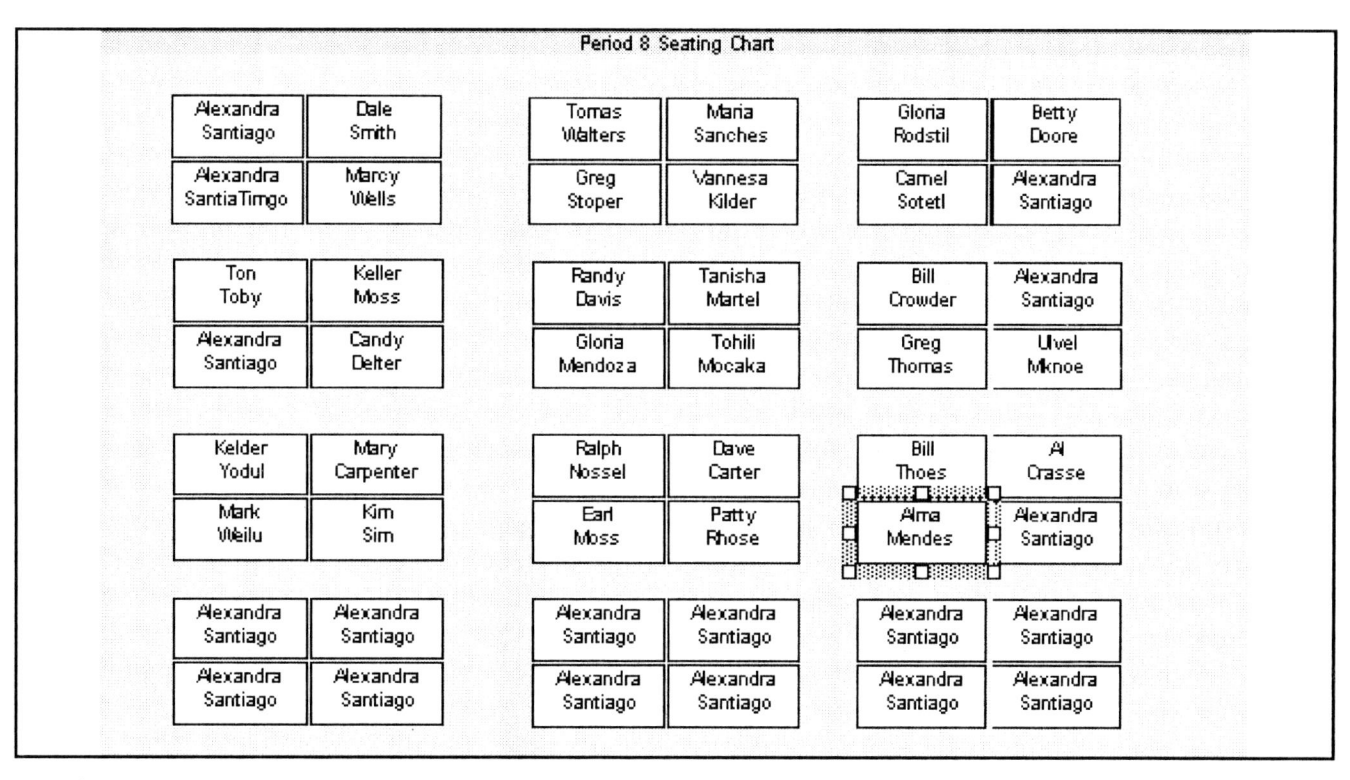

Period 8 Seating Chart

Alexandra Santiago	Dale Smith	Tomas Walters	Maria Sanches	Gloria Rodstil	Betty Doore
Alexandra SantiaTimgo	Marcy Wells	Greg Stoper	Vannesa Kilder	Camel Sotetl	Alexandra Santiago
Ton Toby	Keller Moss	Randy Davis	Tanisha Martel	Bill Crowder	Alexandra Santiago
Alexandra Santiago	Candy Delter	Gloria Mendoza	Tohili Mocaka	Greg Thomas	Ulvel Mknoe
Kelder Yodul	Mary Carpenter	Ralph Nossel	Dave Carter	Bill Thoes	Al Crasse
Mark Weilu	Kim Sim	Earl Moss	Patty Rhose	Alma Mendes	Alexandra Santiago
Alexandra Santiago	Alexandra Santiago	Alexandra Santiago	Alexandra Santiago	Alexandra Santiago	Alexandra Santiago
Alexandra Santiago	Alexandra Santiago	Alexandra Santiago	Alexandra Santiago	Alexandra Santiago	Alexandra Santiago

Excel Seating Charts 2 (Template File Name: Seating Chart Groups 2.xlt)

Student Templates for Microsoft Excel

Math Workbook Spreadsheet

The Math Workbook worksheets are designed for teachers to either print out or to have students work directly on the computer. Teachers can create dozens of worksheets from one template. They can also use the computer as an automatic corrector by having students enter their scores from their paper into the corresponding work sheet on the computer to verify the results.

The math worksheets are organized into Addition, Subtraction, Multiplication and Division worksheets. There is also a collection of three separate workbooks with basic addition facts, using clip art as a teaching tool. Teachers can delete, add, or change the clip art to generate additional spreadsheets.

A happy face is generated in the yellow box if the answer is correct, offering immediate feedback to students. An incorrect answer will receive no happy face. In the top right corner, a total score is given and a percentage is generated from the total number of problems attempted. Teachers can review these answers with the class using an overhead projector. They can also have students create their own problems for their peers to solve.

The main worksheets are pictured below and on the following page. Five additional worksheets are available on the CD-ROM.

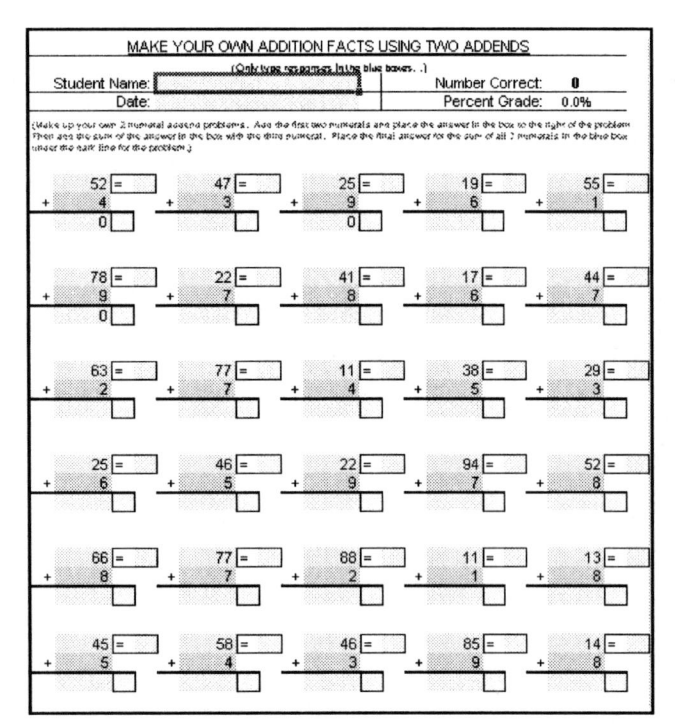

Math Worksheet: Addition (Template File Name: Addition.xlt)

Math Level 1—Subtraction (Template File Name: Subtraction.xlt)

#2771 Teachers' Template Collection for Microsoft Office © Teacher Created Resources, Inc.

Student Templates for Microsoft Excel

Student Templates *(cont.)*

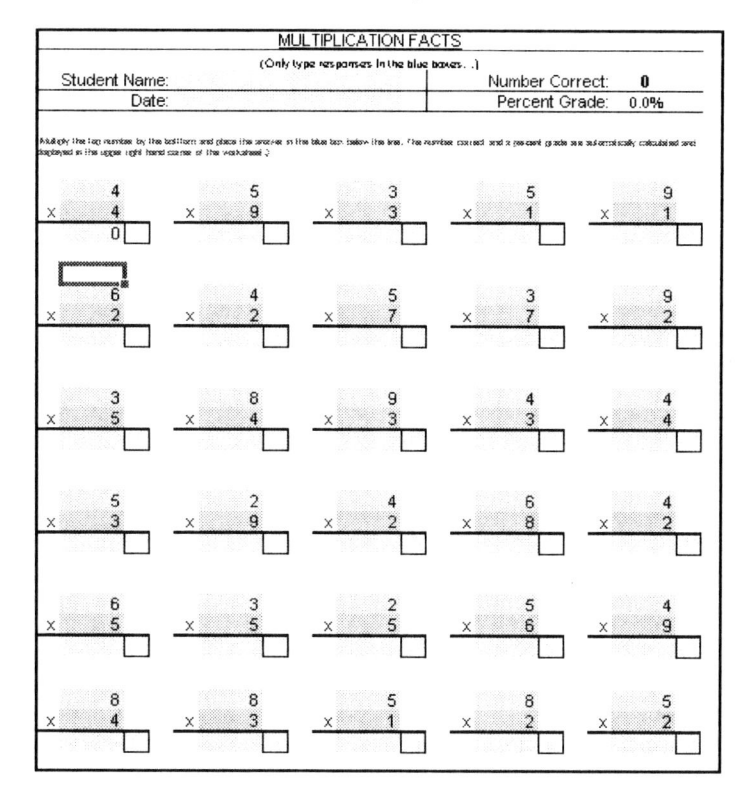

Math Worksheet: Multiplication (Template File Name: Multiplication.xlt)

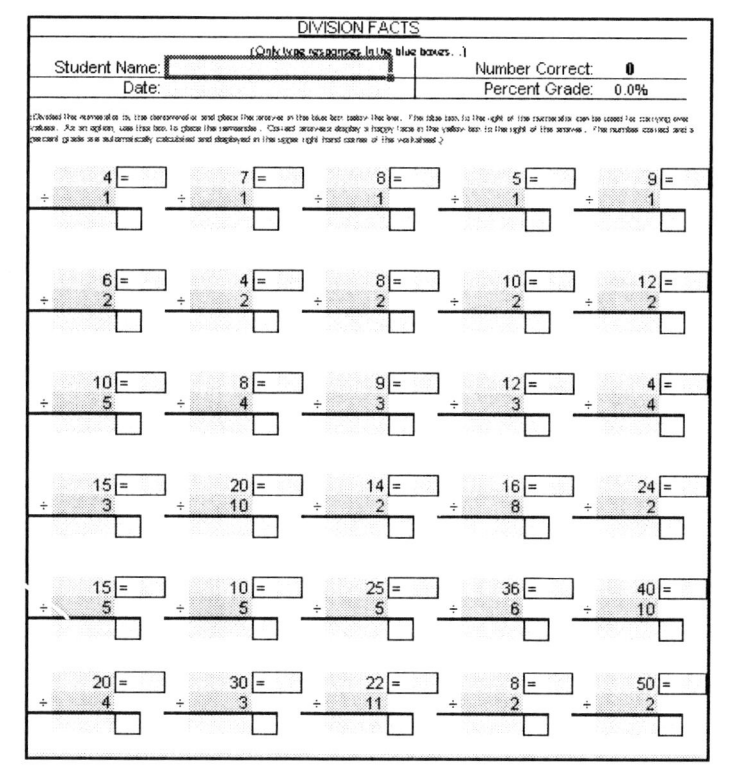

Math Worksheet: Division (Template File Name: Division.xlt)

© *Teacher Created Resources, Inc.* *101* #2771 *Teachers' Template Collection for Microsoft Office*

Student Templates for Microsoft Excel

Student Templates *(cont.)*

Student Planner

To use the Student Planner, click into any of the cell areas and begin typing. The layout of the planner worksheet is designed to follow each day in a school year's calendar. Date formulas are built in to allow for the dates to automatically appear.

To edit the start date,

- Click on cell K1 for the day value.
- Click on cell K2 for the year value.

Features and Benefits:

1. Students can plan collaboratively with their teachers and peers.
2. Parents will have a better understanding of what is happening at school as students share their weekly planning calendars and schedules.
3. Students will be able to create portfolios of their schoolwork and have a stake in their education.
4. It provides a valuable learning experience which teaches students to set goals, evaluate their work, and take greater responsibility for their own learning.

Student Planner (Template File Name: Student Planner.xlt)

Teacher Templates for Microsoft Access

School Information System (Windows Only)

Microsoft Access will unleash the power of *Microsoft Office* by allowing administrators to organize student schedules and class size rosters with the click of a mouse. The *Student Information System* can create student phone lists as well as document student activity. This program can be run on a network.

Key Features:

- Manage student schedules.
- Create student and faculty lists.
- View class size quickly by class or instructor.
- Review students' status and make quick adjustments.

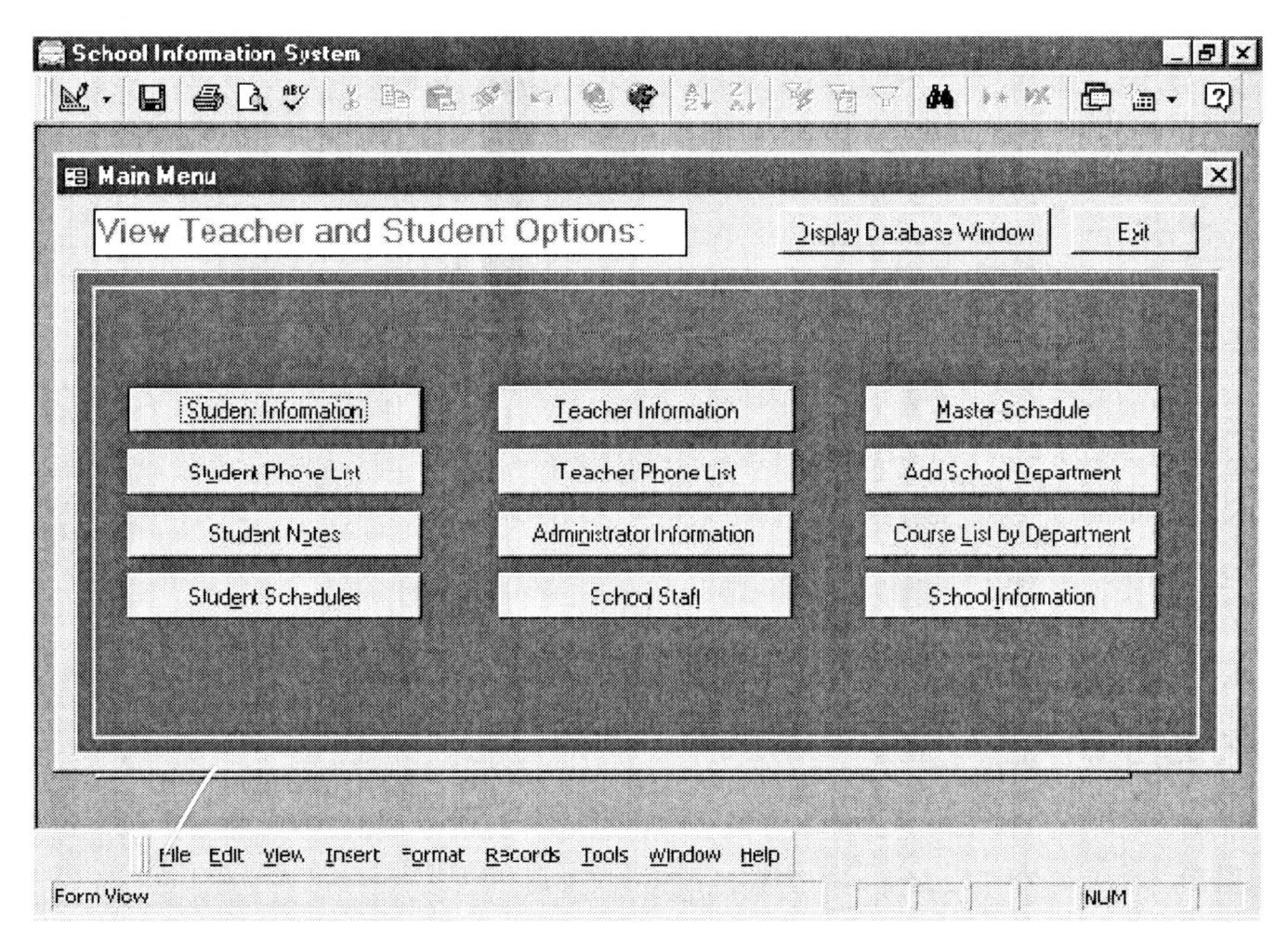

Student Information System (Opening Screen. File Name: School Information Database.mdb)

© Teacher Created Resources, Inc.

Teacher Templates for Microsoft Access

School Information System *(cont.)*

Teacher Information Sample Screen

Teacher Templates for Microsoft Access

School Information System *(cont.)*

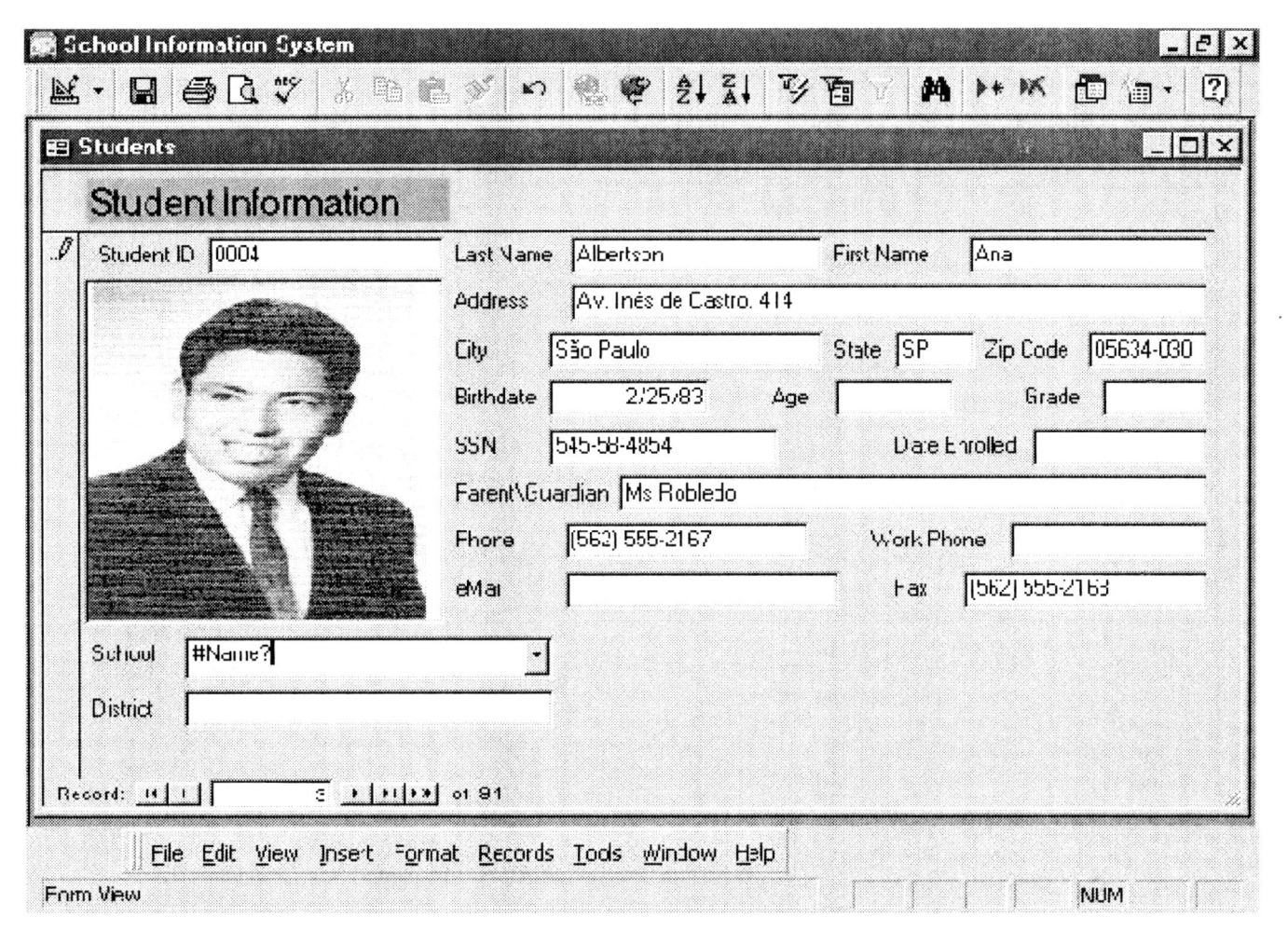

Student Information Sample Screen

Teacher Templates for Microsoft Access

School Information System *(cont.)*

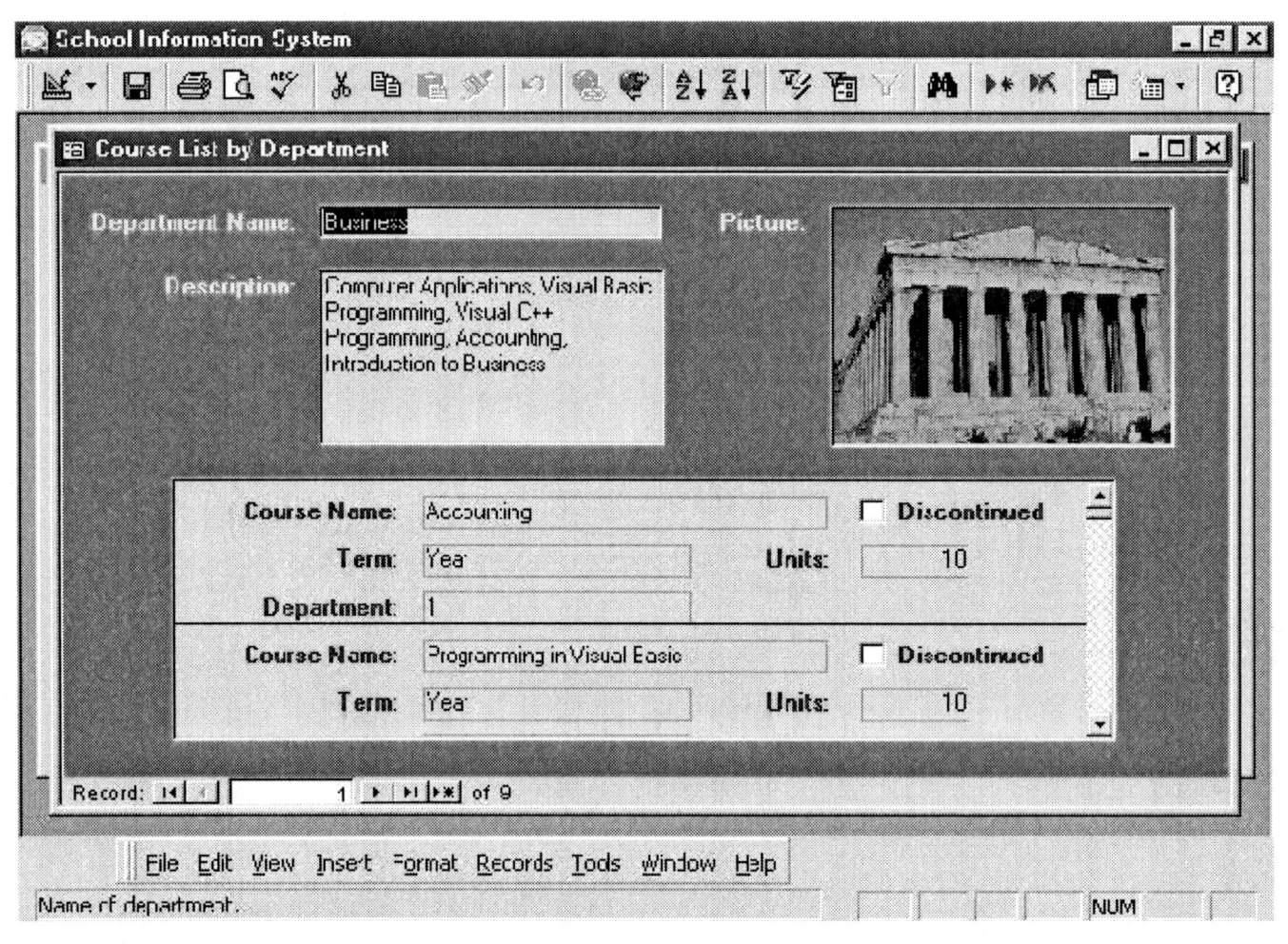

Course By Department Sample Screen

#2771 Teachers' Template Collection for Microsoft Office   106   © *Teacher Created Resources, Inc.*

Teacher Templates for Microsoft Access

School Information System *(cont.)*

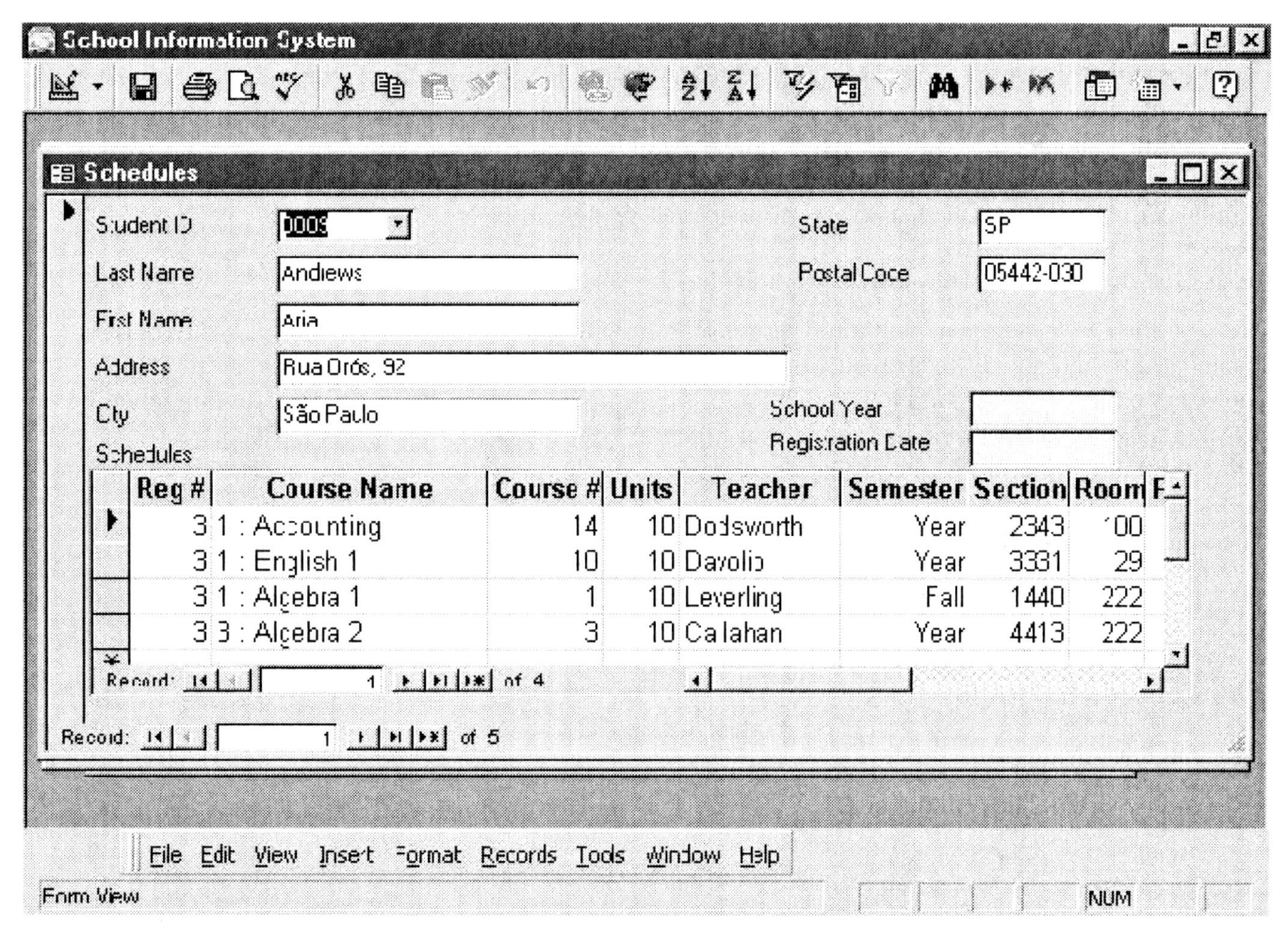

Student Schedule Sample Screen

Teacher Templates for Microsoft Binder

Microsoft Binder (Windows Only)

The *Microsoft Binder* program is an ideal way of holding documents, spreadsheets and presentations in a single "binder." From this binder a teacher or student can view a variety of screens that are organized based on individual needs. Teachers can create multiple folders for each student and send templates from a binder to a particular folder. Teachers can organize all their files in their binder and not have to open another folder. Our sample teacher binder includes all the necessary templates to get started in the classroom. Teachers can create and save new documents into their binder. The Student binder includes templates that will make the learning experience more engaging.

To use the *Binder*, follow these steps:

Click on the *Binder* template and the *Binder* program will open a screen with a variety of templates located on the left side of the screen. To open a template, scroll on the arrows on the bottom left of your screen until you will find an application of your choice. Select the template by double-clicking on it. Any template that is located in a binder is called a "Section." In order to print, save as, or copy a section go to the **Section** menu on the menu bar and highlight your choice. To import a new template or document into your binder, go to section on the menu bar and select ***Add from File*** from the menu. The section menu will also allow you to rearrange your templates that are on display.

The Binder files are named as followed on the CD-ROM:

- Maps Binder.obt
- Science Binder.obt
- Student Awards Binder.obt
- Student Templates Binder.obt
- Teacher Templates Binder.obt

Index of CD-ROM File Names

Activity	File Name	Page Number
Introduction Presentation File	Introduction Presentation File	
Language Arts and Reading Folder		
Word Templates		
Daily Journal	Daily Journal.dot	44
My Story	My Story.dot	47
Personal Journal	Personal Journal.dot	44
PowerPoint Templates		
A Day at the Zoo	A Day at the Zoo.pot	79
Family Tree	Family Tree.pot	77
Storybook Maker	Storybook Maker.pot	81
Math Folder		
Excel Templates		
AdditionAddition.xlt		100
Division	Division.xlt	101
Math Level A	Math Level A 1.xlt	Not shown
	Math Level A 2.xlt	Not shown
	Math Level A 3.xlt	Not shown
Math Level B	Math Level B.xlt	Not shown
Math Level C	Math Level C.xlt	Not shown
Multiplication	Multiplication.xlt	101
Subtraction	Subtraction.xlt	100
Science Folder		
Word Templates		
Science Anatomy Lungs	Science Anatomy Lungs.dot	54
	Science Anatomy Lungs 2.dot	54
Science Anatomy Brain	Science Anatomy Brain.dot	52
	Science Anatomy Brain 2.dot	52
Science Anatomy Digestive	Science Anatomy Digestive.dot	53
	Science Anatomy Digestive 2.dot	53
Science Anatomy Hand	Science Anatomy Hand.dot	51
Science Anatomy Heart	Science Anatomy Heart.dot	55
	Science Anatomy Heart 2.dot	55
Science Anatomy Skull	Science Anatomy Skull.dot	56
Science Computer Technology	Science Computer Technology.dot	57
	Science Computer Technology 2.dot	57
Science Environment	Science Environment.dot	56
Science Instruments Microscope	Science Instruments Microscope.dot	58
	Science Instruments Microscope 2.dot	58
Science Liquids	Science Liquids.dot	60
Science Molecules	Science Molecules 1.dot	59
	Science Molecules 2.dot	59
Science Rocket Technology	Science Rocket Technology.dot	60
Science Space Exploration	Science Space Exploration 2.dot	61
	Science Space Exploration 3.dot	61
Scientific Instruments	Scientific Instruments.dot	62
PowerPoint Templates		
Marine Biology	Marine Biology.pot	74

Index of CD-ROM File Names *(cont.)*

Activity	File name	Page Number
Seating Charts Folder		
Word Templates		
Seating Chart A	Seating Chart A.dot	9
Seating Chart B	Seating Chart B.dot	10
Seating Chart C	Seating Chart C.dot	10
Seating Chart D	Seating Chart D.dot	11
Seating Chart E	Seating Chart E.dot	11
Seating Chart F	Seating Chart F.dot	12
Seating Chart G	Seating Chart G.dot	12
Seating Chart H	Seating Chart H.dot	Not shown
Excel Templates		
Seating Chart Groups 1	Seating Chart Groups 1.xlt	99
Seating Chart Groups 2	Seating Chart Groups 2.xlt	99
Social Studies Folder		
Word Templates		
Africa Map 1	Africa Map 1.dot	32
Africa Map 2	Africa Map 2.dot	32
Africa Map 3	Africa Map 3.dot	32
Australia Map 1	Australia Map 1.dot	33
Australia Map 2	Australia Map 2.dot	33
Europe & Asia Map 1	Europe & Asia Map 1.dot	34
Europe & Asia Map 2	Europe & Asia Map 2.dot	34
Geotest 1	Geotest 1.dot	31
Geotest 2	Geotest 2.dot	31
Globe Map 1	Globe Map 1.dot	37
Globe Map 2	Globe Map 2.dot	37
Globe Map 3	Globe Map 3.dot	37
Globe Map 4	Globe Map 4.dot	37
Mexico Map 1	Mexico Map 1.dot	35
Mexico Map 2	Mexico Map 2.dot	35
North America Map 1	North America Map 1.dot	31
North America Map 2	North America Map 2.dot	31
South America Map 1	South America Map 1.dot	36
South America Map 2	South America Map 2.dot	36
United States Map 1	United States Map 1.dot	38
United States Map 2	United States Map 2.dot	38
United States Map 3	United States Map 3.dot	38
Voyages to the Past Africa 1	Voyages to the Past Africa 1.dot	40
Voyages to the Past Africa 2	Voyages to the Past Africa 2.dot	40
Voyages to the Past Europe 1	Voyages to the Past Europe 1.dot	41
Voyages to the Past Europe 2	Voyages to the Past Europe 2.dot	41
Voyages to the Past North America 1	Voyages to the Past North America 1.dot	42
Voyages to the Past North America 2	Voyages to the Past North America 2.dot	42
Voyages to the Past Asia 1	Voyages to the Past Asia 1.dot	39
World Map 1	World Map 1.dot	
PowerPoint Templates		
Social Science	Social Science.pot	75

Index of CD-ROM File Names (cont.)

Activity	File name	Page Number
Student Awards Templates Folder		
Word Templates		
Artist of the Month	Artist of the Month(L).dot	13
	Artist of the Month.dot	13
Athlete of the Month	Athlete of the Month(L).dot	16
	Athlete of the Month.dot	16
Book Monitor	Book Monitor(L).dot	16
	Book Monitor.dot	16
Citizenship	Citizenship(L).dot	17
	Citizenship.dot	17
Library Helper	Library Helper(L).dot	15
	Library Helper.dot	15
Perfect Attendance	Perfect Attendance(L).dot	14
	Perfect Attendance.dot	14
Principal's Student of the Month	Principal's Student of the Month(L).dot	18
	Principal's Student of the Month.dot	18
Speller of the Month	Speller of the Month(L).dot	18
	Speller of the Month.dot	18
Student Athlete of the Month	Student Athlete of the Month.dot	Not shown
Student Helper of the Month	Student Helper of the Month(L).dot	19
	Student Helper of the Month.dot	19
Student of the Month	Student of the Month(L).dot	17
	Student of the Month.dot	17
The Big Cheese	The Big Cheese(L).dot	20
	The Big Cheese.dot	20
PowerPoint Templates		
Student Awards Collection	Student Awards Collection.pot	69
Student Information Database Folder		
School Information Database (Windows)	School Information Database.mdb	103
Student Templates Folder		
Word Templates		
Daily Schedule	Daily Schedule.dot	46
Student Report 1	Student Report 1.dot	48
Student Report 2	Student Report 2.dot	49
Study Buddies	Study Buddies.dot	50
Vocabulary Wordlist	Vocabulary Wordlist.dot	45
Excel Templates		
Student Planner	Student Planner.xlt	102
PowerPoint Templates		
Study Guide	Study Guide.pot	83

Index of CD-ROM File Names *(cont.)*

Activity	File name	Page Number
Teacher Tools Folder		
Word Templates		
Classroom Inventory	Classroom Inventory.dot	21
Classroom Management	Classroom Management.dot	22
Class Supply List	Class Supply List.dot	23
Discipline Notice	Discipline Notice.dot	24
Homework Assignments	Homework Assignments.dot	25
Ideas for Substitute	Ideas for Substitute.dot	29
Letter Head	Letter Head.dot	26
Letter Head 2	Letter Head 2.dot	26
Memo	Memo.dot	27
Memo 2	Memo 2.dot	27
Memo 3	Memo 3.dot	Not Shown
Notes for Substitute	Notes for Substitute.dot	29
School Rules	School Rules.dot	24
Student Trip Slip	Student Trip Slip.dot	23
Teacher Cards	Teacher Cards.dot	28
Teacher Cards 1	Teacher Cards 1.dot	28
Teacher Cards 2	Teacher Cards 2.dot	Not Shown
Week at a Glance	Week at a Glance.dot	30
Excel Templates		
Grade Book Deluxe	Grade Book Deluxe.xlt	95
Lesson Planner	Lesson Planner.xlt	98
PowerPoint Templates		
Open House 2	Open House 2.pot	65
Social Science Department Info	Social Science Department Info.pot	72
The Electronic Yearbook	The Electronic Yearbook.pot	86
Binder Templates (Windows Only)		
Maps Binder	Maps Binder.obt	108
Science Binder	Science Binder.obt	108
Student Awards Binder	Student Awards Binder.obt	108
Student Templates Binder	Student Templates Binder.obt	108
Teacher Templates Binder	Teacher Templates Binder.obt	108